CAUSES AND EFFECTS

Unearthing the Root Causes of the Environmental and Developmental Crises in Africa

DR. PHILIP BHEBHE

CgHope Publications | ZIMBABWE
2020

ISBN 978-1-77929-279-7

EAN 9781779292797

Causes & Effects: Unearthing the Root Causes of the Environmental and Developmental Crises in Africa by Dr. Philip Bhebhe

Email: cghopepublications@outlook.com

Call: +263 (0) 783 484 266
+263 (0) 778 144 260

Published by CgHope Publications in Bulawayo, Zimbabwe.

Printed by Amazon Kindle Direct Publishing.

Layout, design and illustrations by XK Graphics.

This book is dedicated to all those yearning to see Africa rising out of crises; those who are passionate enough to seek and share the way out, for the sake of the current and all the future generations.

CAUSES AND

EFFECTS

Unearthing the Root Causes of the Environmental and Developmental Crises in Africa

Dr. Philip Bhebhe

Typesetting: Yenah Silape
Design & Layout: XK Graphics
Further Editing & Proofreading: Batsirai Ziyavaya

ACKNOWLEDGMENTS

With special thanks:

To my daughters, Sinothando and Carol, for filling my life with joy and giving me so much to pray for.

To my sons, Hubert and Harris, for their vision for this book and their hearts for concerned parents everywhere who are worried about the future of Africa.

To my son-in-law, Darren, for wishing me success in everything I do, and for his love and kindness.

To my daughters-in-law, Thandeka and Kudzai, for not forgetting me when I moved to Gweru and for deeming this project valuable enough to commit it in theirs prayers every day.

To my grandchildren: Jaden, Tariana, Andiswa, Khanyisa, Lindo and Zothile, for being lovely and always making it a joy to speak to them. Jaden has become a prolific author of children's books at the age of eleven years!

To my wife, Nyengeterai, for her love and willingness to spend countless hours with me over the last forty-five years, covering our children in prayer and advising me that working hard does not kill.

To my typesetter, Yenah Silape, for preparing this book's manuscript for publishing and for encouraging me that this work is not only going to benefit Africa, but the whole world.

To all those that I consulted in order to come out with a well-balanced and stimulating book.

To my Masters' students at Midlands State University for the encouragement.

To Shonhiwa, I say, thank you for your input.

Finally, to the Almighty God for giving me strength, wisdom and zeal.

TABLE OF CONTENTS

CHAPTER FOUR

CHAPTER FIVE

CHAPTER SIX

INTRODUCTION

"As we confront the often troubled relationship between 'man' and nature, we must be ecologically and economically realistic and we must take into consideration cultural restraints."

-Harold J. Coolidge, 1983.

Africa, the second largest continent in the world, covering 11.7 million square miles (30.3 square kilometers), and the cradle of human beings and civilization (Mazrui p.61) is in a crisis. The causes of socio-political turbulence, economic difficulties, environmental degradation, and its cultural dislocation have been documented (Nyerere 1985; Mazrui 1986; M'Mwereria 1990 and 1991; and Mkangi 1990). Yet, action to redress these problems and reverse the trend has so far not produced the expected results.

The escalating degradation of agricultural lands, the destruction of rainforests, the increasing biodiversity losses, and uncontrolled urban, industrial and rural population growth are a living testimony of the crisis. These pose a great challenge to the future of the African human community.

Pressure is rising on governments, Non-Governmental Organizations (NGOs), and communities to protect the environment and introduce sustainable development. However, in the face of the unjust international economic order and internal continental contradictions, there is a little progress (if any is made). Lip-service measures (react and cure prescriptions), and the pursuance of unsustainable development strategies, which are neither African nor European, have come to occupy the center stage. These measures prove to be self-defeating in the long-term.

There is now an urgent need to bridge the gulf of perceptions, and the gap between political pronouncements and deeds, if future generations of Africa are to have a place on this continent and in the rest of the world. In this context, let the truth be told and action taken now to avoid the looming catastrophe. Let Africa be warned: nature takes its time to cut human beings to their size; but when it hits, its effects are devastating. The signs of that looming fate are becoming more visible day-by-day.

A new orientation towards nature, based on fundamental changes in the value systems, norms, attitudes, and life-styles is imperative for survival and continuity. This should be accompanied by radical change in institutional structures and policies.

Financial Resources

Additional resources are required and will be necessary to finance the adherence to certain costly principles of Agenda 21. The United Nations must ensure access to developing countries to the additional financial resources, which they will require to integrate the environmental dimensions into their own developmental policies and practices. Moreover, ensure financial resources in the incremental costs that will be incurred in complying with the international environmental conventions and protocols.

Bearing in mind that financial constraints have been one of the major hindrances of development in Africa and the rest of the Less Economically Developed Countries (LEDCs), Africa must now articulate its thinking on the environment and sustainable development. The continent must spare no efforts to put its vision on alternative initiatives as well as action plans on the bargaining table of the United Nations Conference on Environment and Development (UNCED).

Africa in collaboration with other Less Economically Developed Countries (LEDCs), must take full advantage of its 'new found power' concealed in her 'recognized natural resources'. This should help Africa bargain for the resources necessary to implement internal environmental conventions and protocols, which will help the continent, achieve sustainable development in the long run. For the rich in the North, this is a decisive test for their commitment to funding a noble cause for the benefit of all.

Technology Transfer

The developing countries, in particular, should be given access to environmentally sound technologies on an equitable and affordable basis.
Africa should not wait for the West to introduce her to the kind of technology that is environmentally sound and needed. It should take the lead through African expertise and Non-Governmental Organizations (NGOs) to identify a kind of technology that is culturally feasible. Succinctly, African representatives should emphasize technology transfer.

Strengthening of Institutions

The need to strengthen institutions such as the United Nations Environmental Programme (UNEP) and the United Nations Development Programme (UNDP) is long overdue. Part of this strengthening should include ways of ensuring communication and collaboration between the environment and development.

In addition to these global structures, grass-root formal and informal groups and organizations, NGOs, governments and semi-government institutions or agencies at local and national level should also be strengthened. It is further suggested that linkages among, and between these institutions and the United Nations' bodies should be established where they do not exist and strengthened where they do.

After outlining and suggesting Africa's priorities, it is now imperative to analyze the problems of environmental destruction, pollution, biodiversity loss and sustainable development to bring to light, the main cause of the present crisis. It is only after fully understanding the nature of the crisis that practical recommendations to resolve the problems can be suggested.

Nearly all African countries have research action programs, lobbying at both national and international levels to awaken the public to environmental issues and sustainable development. However, little has been done to educate the masses on the basic, underlying and immediate causes of the present environmental and developmental problems.

Despite the numerous efforts to correct this complex situation, the results are evidently poor and this is without surprise, because the cart has been put before the horse; hence, progress has been difficult and frustrating. The fact that Africa is in a serious environmental and developmental crisis is no longer a gossip, but a reality that manifests itself in many forms.

The land reform in Zimbabwe is a good example of such a crisis. People have gone into farms, cut down trees, hunted down livestock and destroyed infrastructure. As a result, the breadbasket of Africa has now become a basket case. Despite all this, it is only the effects or symptoms of the crisis and not the causes that are commonly known or at least emphasized. The basic and the underlying causes of Africa's environmental and developmental crisis and their cumulative effects on human beings and biodiversity are summarized in the diagram below.

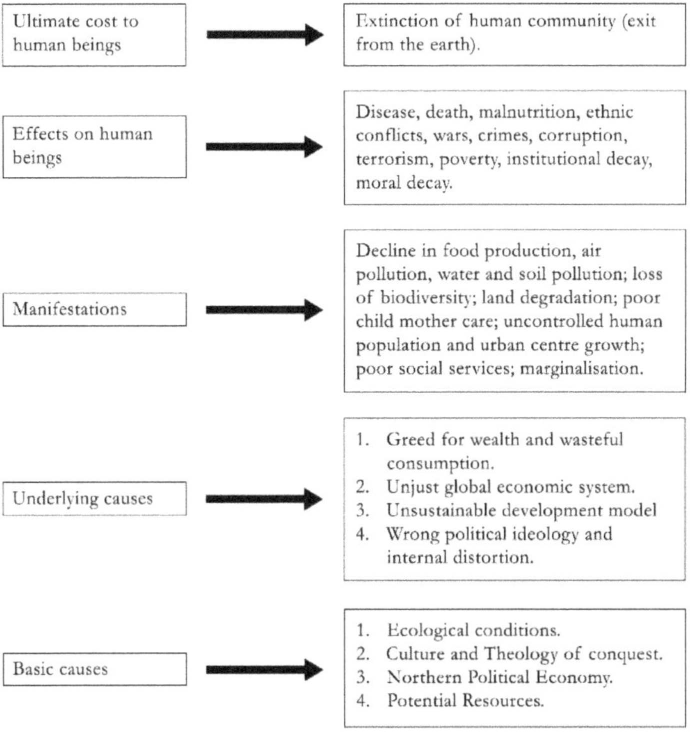

Figure 1. Causes and cumulative effects of environmental destruction and unsustainable politico-economic model.

The most oppressive constraints to environmental protection, sustainability and improvement of the quality of life of the African people can be traced to the current unfair economic disorder, imbalanced political ideologies and internal contradictions. Escalating environmental degradation, seen through food shortages, poor health systems, soil erosion, catchment area deforestation, desertification and the minatory climatic change are partly the products of those constraints.

Africa's own internal contradictions include the institution of reckless political decisions and unexamined policies such as the Indigenization policy in Zimbabwe. Others include policies such as the establishment of environmentally unfriendly projects, viz. citing hydroelectric dams in wrong places, establishment of coffee or tea zones in water catchment areas, environmentally laissez-faire attitudes; to 'inciting' ethnic and tribal conflicts, or civil wars; premeditated capital flight, mismanagement of institutions, locked-in-thinking by the elites to corruption.

Such practices themselves bring social unrest and may create instability in governments, thus further crippling Africa's capacity to tackle environmental issues and to embark on sustainable development.

Today, nearly all African governments have resorted to management by crisis as a method of running the affairs of the state. The next stage may be the continent's crash landing if nothing is done to reverse the current trend.

Professor Ali Mazrui summarized the basic underlying causes of the African crisis in terms of the influence of what he called the triple heritage (i.e. the indigenous culture, the coming of Islam and Western traditions). He says, *"The introduction of capitalism and the cash economy have produced disastrous results. Africans no longer hold nature in awe; they hold it in avarice and profit. The influence of the triple heritage is not confined to the current conflict between human beings and nature, it is presented also in the tensions between city and countryside, between soldiers and politicians, between elite and the masses, between religious and the secular, between longing for autonomy and the shackles of dependency upon imported culture,"* (Mazrui, 1986).

The destruction of what is basic to all African cultures closes the relationship between human beings and nature. This has opened the Pandora box which Africa's western style institutions and structures of authority are now incapable of closing.

Our continent's environmental and developmental complex problems cannot continue to be tackled by the traditional piece-meal approaches. They require integrated and multidisciplinary approaches that synthesize indigenous knowledge, and culture, mobilize institutions, economic, human, natural and organizational resources from grass-root to national levels. This is not the time for political pronouncements, but action.

The challenge for national governments; NGOs; local, bilateral and multilateral agencies is to work more closely with each other in a more coordinated manner to achieve the cherished goals. This must be done with full understanding of the historical circumstances as well as the local and international factors responsible for Africa's environment and development debacle. In times of crisis, let us always remember to tackle the root cause(s) if we will ever have lasting solutions and not deal with the symptoms for short-term bluff. The latter remedy, on which a lot of time, energy and resources are wasted, seems to be the trend in many African countries today.

CHAPTER ONE

COLONIAL LEGACY

AND LOSS OF AFRICAN BIODIVERSITY

"It is ever more apparent that humanity has been living with a grand delusion: that we can go on consuming the planet's resources forever."

-John Laird, 1991

1.1 Pre-colonial Setting and Preservation of African Natural Heritage

Prior to the advent of Islam and European influences, indigenous African cultural, and religious traditions promoted a system that allowed mutual co-existence between human beings and nature with God in between. There was a good deal of a culture of co-habitation and co-pasturing (Mazrui, 1986), which promoted co-existence of human beings, and animals in close proximity and within the same compound. It was unexceptional for pastoral people with large herds of livestock to sleep among their animals.

Indeed, the first traces of agriculture in Egypt, the cradle of human civilization, date back to about 12500 B.C. with indications of plant cultivation and animal husbandry (von Malydell, 1987). Game hunting was very selective. For example, large-scale hunting was restricted for dry seasons when most animals were mature and off their breeding periods. It was a common practice to release young animals when captured. If a pregnant female was killed, it could have only been unintentional. This traditional practice of game cropping ensured sustainability and preservation of species.

Seasoned or professional hunters were skillful wildlife ecologists. They knew the breeding cycle of different animal species, their feeding habits, and their daily and seasonal movements. Habitats of birds were linked with the various layers of shrubs and trees' canopy. The people made sure these canopy structures were not destroyed.

The practice of shifting cultivation was based on established ideals and obligations other than avarice and profit, as is the case today. This old and self-regenerating agricultural practice embraced culture as well as the moral, and socioeconomic and political demands of society, whose organization considered land not as a private property, but as the basis of community life. Hence, all the community members through allocation shared land by traditional institutions of authority such as chiefs in Zimbabwe.

Equitable distribution of land among the members of the community was the guiding principle. It was considered immoral at that time to leave any member of the community landless. Even after sharing the land, if any member experienced crop failure for one reason or another, those with good harvests contributed to the unfortunate members, to see them through to the next harvest.

The cooperative spirit was well entrenched in the African traditional culture. The Biblical spirit of, *"love thy neighbor as thyself,"* was alive and enduring. Africans realized then that the survival of their agricultural civilization depended upon their ability to retain soil fertility. The periodic abandonment of over-cultivated land, and overgrazed areas to allow regeneration of natural vegetation, and rebuilding soil fertility before re-use was a clever practice that promoted soil and vegetation conservation.

The use of animal manure and vegetable waste as sources of organic fertilizer promoted organic farming. The use of nitrogen fixing pulses in mixed cropping, the growing of plants of different growth patterns and maturity duration, helped to stabilize soil fertility and to prevent soil erosion. It was also an effective biological way of managing pests and diseases. It also conserved biodiversity of annual and biannual crops, and plants while reducing labor costs. It was, indeed, an integrated system.

Indigenous Africans also understood plant ecology well. The following picturesque description by the Yorubas of Western Nigeria testifies: *"The plants eat and drink, as it were, not from one table, but from many tables under the same sky,"* (Henry, 1949; Ojo, 1966).

Throughout Africa where cultivation was practiced, tree species were planted alongside crops, annual or perennial, in an intimate combination. Annual crops like finger millet, bulrush millet, beans, simsim, sorghum, maize, groundnuts, peas, and perennial crops like banana, cocoa, coffee, yams, cassava and others were grown under the cover of scattered trees.

A good example is the shifting agriculture still practiced in the Kordofan Province of Sudan, where a multipurpose nitrogen-fixing shrub, Acacia Senegal is used extensively. The use of the gum-arabic producing tree in a gum-cropping cycle represents a planned fertility-building exercise by the local community. After a gum production cycle, the acacia trees are cut down and allowed to coppice during the cropping cycle. This lasts until the yields of groundnuts, sorghum and bulrush millet begins to decline.

Once the last crops are harvested, the Acacia Senegal is allowed to regenerate and grow into gum producing trees. They are then left to produce gum-arabic for a known number of years. At the same time, the trees rebuild soil fertility through nitrogen fixation, and mineralization of dead leaves before the cycle starts again (Skerman, 1977). The scope of trees and shrubs both in sustaining soil productivity is therefore not new to Africans as has been suggested by some scientists.

The point being stressed here is that the indigenous African people practiced what has now come to be known as mixed or intercropping and agro-forestry respectively, long before the introduction of the exploitative Western agricultural practices. Trees were an integral part of the farming system as soil fertility builders, sources of fuelwood, sources of building materials and as animal feeds.

Shifting cultivation, intercropping, agroforestry and long rotational crop-livestock systems embodied in indigenous agriculture, represented unique efforts by peasant Africans to manage, and protect their environment and biodiversity. Reckless destruction of forests was not allowed. Trees for building purposes were carefully selected and only one or a few would be cut from one stump or spot as the case would be. Fuelwood was collected from dead trees or branches and of trees harvested for other purposes.

Besides being environmentally conscious, and following simple but environmentally friendly agriculture and game cropping practices, the indigenous Africans have had a wealth of knowledge about plant characteristics. The knowledge ranged from their food value to the medicinal properties of plants. They knew their quality for building, furniture, and handcraft materials to their soil conservation capacity and related uses. The earlier African practitioners of shifting agriculture exchanged and preserved germplasm.

It was a common practice to collect new varieties and species of plants during visits to other geographical areas. In addition, elders had an eye for quality seeds to be kept from a harvest for the next planting season. People's traditional food norms, cultural and religious beliefs and taboos, have always played a part in indigenous efforts towards environmental protection and biodiversity conservation.

For example, Africans would not eat meat from their totems such as Shiri (for bird) Siziba or Hove (for fish) Nkomo (for cattle), Ndlovu (elephant) Dube (for zebra) etc. Were these not efficient conservation measures? It is important to incorporate some of these time-tested technologies and indigenous knowledge in technological modernization for efficient resource management.

The pertinent or burning questions are: "if the traditional forms of silvopastoral and agro-silvopastoral practices were environmentally friendly; what factors brought about the misuse of land, the result of which are soil degradation, deforestation, food insecurity, adverse climatic conditions and desertification? What caused the disruption of the ancient intelligent and sometimes instinctive methods of protecting the environment and its biodiversity? What forced our people to cultivate marginal lands such as steep slopes, arid areas and build in flood-prone areas? How has the shortage of fuel-wood come about?"

The reasons commonly given are fast population growth combined with wrong or inappropriate technologies and limited access to arable land. True, the increasing human, and livestock population and growing cultural demands are the immediate causes of increasing pressure on natural resources. Nevertheless, they are not the basic causes. For a large continent with vast resources like Africa, its present population should pose no immediate environment or development crisis.

African policy-makers have bought the thesis that population pressure on land, and available infrastructures, and facilities in urban centers is one of the root causes of the continent's environmental degradation and pollution. As a result, every country has gone full thrust in family planning. The present development strategies, control over land and lifestyle certainly make such a move sensible.

However, are we facing the truth? A quick glance at the continent shows that Africa is under populated compared to other continents. In addition, the continent has vast natural resources, which can meet the needs of the growing population. Take for example Tanzania, it has a population of about 51.04 million people and yet the country is bigger than France, Germany and Spain combined. A similar situation can be said of the Sudan, Democratic Republic of Congo and other countries.

A World Bank Report of 1986 estimated that a small country with a fertile land as Uganda with a population of less than 14 million people at that time could comfortably support 60 million people. How then does the question of population pressure come in? The answer is simple: corruption, unequal distribution of wealth, poor development strategies, and governance issues and poor planning in urban centers. Correct these anomalies and Africa will discover it has been dancing to the wrong tune.

Nevertheless, there is a need to monitor population trends to ensure that its growth is in line with the rate of development. With improved health care and reduced child mortality rate, Malthusianism is real and must not be overlooked. Of note, is the fact that the basic and underlying causes of Africa's development and environment crises are either deliberately ignored or de-emphasized?

If the present generation of Africans has been and is destroying the continent's environment and accelerating the loss of biodiversity, then Prof. Ali Mazrui's words may be true: *"they have made a treaty with colonial legacy, which is essentially destructive, and disloyal to ancient practices and to the principle of indigenous authenticity,"* (Mazrui, 1986). The major features of this treaty are unsustainable development models, consumerism mentality and greed for wealth.

The root-cause of Africa's economic under development, environmental problems and cultural dislocation is represented by the interplay of three underlying factors. The continent's ecology, climate, abundant but fragile resources, and the political economy of imperialism, ecosystems, climate influenced indigenous cultures and levels of technological development. Plenty of sun, water, mineral wealth and biological diversity all year round meant simple technologies of building, and for protection and cultivation.

The easy and simple life led to the saying: *"There is plenty of time in Africa."* This contrasts significantly with the harsh climatic and ecological conditions of the North, which demanded sophisticated technologies in order to ensure survival. This gave rise to the saying: *"Necessity is the mother of invention."* The harsh environment also gave Europe the culture of conquest and *'planning ahead'* in anticipation of harsh seasons. Out of this *'planning ahead'* came the popular saying: *"Make hay while the sun shines."*

Imperialists took advantage of their superior technologies developed to counter the harsh environment of the Northern Hemisphere to conquer and impose a political economy of imperialism on the African continent that still lived in simplicity. However, it must be noted that Western imperialism was not interested in creating a solid African capitalism that was sustainable. Its main thrust was:

i. Destruction of traditional African cultures and economies.

ii. Transmission of capital greed to Africa without instilling capital discipline in Africans.

iii. Inculcation of profit making motive in the indigenous Africans, but not durable entrepreneurial skills and risk taking necessary for building a solid capitalism.

iv. Infusion of secular materialism in African minds, but not the Western rationale of pursuing it (Prof. Ali Mazrui, 1986).

The impact of these thrusts has been the dis-orientation of African minds as reflected, particularly in the post-independence era by loss of African work ethics, destruction of African culture and resources, mimic change in African lifestyles, institutionalization of corruption, and embezzlement and the promotion of a dependency-syndrome in most spheres of life, in particular political economy. By dancing to the wrong tune, many African leaders, and elites of the post-independence era are largely to blame for the accelerated destruction of the continent's environment and its underdevelopment. This will be given a detailed analysis in the second chapter of this book.

How the philosophy and model of Western development as practiced in Africa and the colonial perception of the African people have contributed to the present deplorable state of Africa's environment and development is analyzed in the section below.

1.2 The Colonialists Attitudes and Unsustainable Development Models.

Why is collective self-reliance elusive in contemporary Africa? Why do contemporary African governments appear to lack the capacity to *'plan ahead'* and instead appear to prefer to management by crisis? There are no simple answers to these questions, but analysis of some historical facts can provide an insight to the genesis of the problems.

The growth of capitalism in Europe was based on the development of the culture of planning and research, which were the products of the European peoples' response to their harsh environment. The necessity to survive in the harsh cold environment was the mother of inventions and the industrial revolution. The heating systems and the wearing of trousers by women in the Northern Hemisphere were a response to the harsh cold environment. The short-term success over nature, and the accompanying religious reforms influenced the capitalist ethos and religious perspectives of Europe.

The important point to note is the impact of that victory on the Europeans' perception of and about life. Henceforth, Western capitalist ethos tended to emphasize the ability of man to control nature. Moreover, the influence of capitalism as a secularizing force made Western religions believe that God had a much less control over man's life than it was believed earlier. These two sets of perceptions influenced the colonialists' attitudes towards Africans.

In particular, they shaped the imperial economic development model, exported it to Africa at the expense of the African way of life. The advent of Western colonialism therefore introduced Africans into a radically different perception of nature, development and God. Since then, the African people have been bewitched by the philosophy of the cornucopias who had and still have faith in post-industrial revolution supremacy over nature, human ingenuity and capacity to control nature.

Thus, apart from the earlier influence of the Semites (Arabs and Jews) on indigenous African cultures, the greatest impact came from the Western world. According to a thesis advanced by Professor Ali Mazrui, the impact of the Western world on Africans came through two broad major events:

a) Through cartography, colonization, racism, racial classifications, fragmentation and imperialism, which awakened Africans to know that they were squeezed into a tight corner with no authority over their ancestral continent and its vast wealth and heritage.

b) Through exportation of sons and daughters of the ancestral continent to the North, the Europeans *dis-africanized* the identity of the inhabitants of the continent (Mazrui 1986 p. 113).

The disorientation of the minds of colonized Africans greatly undermined their indigenous cultural heritage, their capacity for collective self-reliance and couched them into greedy profiteers. Valuable indigenous systems of conserving the continent's biodiversity, prevention of environmental degradation and promotion of sustainability, have since been eroded.

The partitioning of Africa by arbitrary boundaries during the Berlin Conference of 1884-5, which was chaired by the Germany Chancellor Otto Von Bismarck and the resulting scrambling for the continent purely for economic gain, coupled with the establishment of institutions that promoted divide-and-rule practices, fragmented the people of Africa further. Not a single African attended the Conference, but it brought together ethnic groups of different backgrounds into one state and intensified division among the people.

These had the effect in the post-independence era of hampering and weakening Africans' capacity to administer the affairs of their multi-ethnic states that were previously homogenous entities. Not surprisingly, the new artificial independent African states at independence had not matured enough to build solid bases that could support sustainable development. The many ethnic and civil wars in the continent can be explained as resulting from the Berlin Conference.

From the European point of view, the fragmentation was a blessing. It provided an enabling environment for multinational companies to exploit cheap African labor, and the abundant natural resources. This helped Western industrial development in the North and the resulting affluent-society. The large numbers of Africans migrating to Europe today are following their money siphoned from their countries by multinational companies.

The destruction of indigenous institutions and the structure of the authority of the elders by the colonial powers undermined the pride, and prestige of the local rulers and their people. The top-bottom approach to administration and development under colonial over lordship that ignored people's wealth of experience and wisdom about their environment further undermined the confidence of indigenous Africans and their leaders.

With their traditional powers removed, the elders could no longer enforce environmental protection measures according to indigenous rules. That marked the beginning of the present rural environmental crisis. Thus, the deliberate policy was designed to tame Africans into submission and to change their political processes. The negative effect of this encouraged environmental degradation and the phenomenon of socio-economic dependency.

Of direct consequences for Africa's physical environment, biodiversity, and level of pollution was the imposition on a tropical people and ecosystems of a political economy of imperialism based on temperate experiences. The introduction of a monoculture agriculture system in fragile ecological areas of Africa encouraged soil erosion; while the introduction of imported plants such as mangoes, paw-paws, bananas, gumtrees etc. led to the loss of well adapted indigenous plant species, which had supported life for centuries and were part of the traditional self-regenerating system of agriculture.

The phenomenon of economic dependency in Africa started with the reduction of the continent to a source of raw materials for the European textile mills. This marked the beginning of the process of incorporating Africa into a global economic system. Since then, Africa has never regained its traditional collective self-reliance in food production and because of the instituted process of marginalization; it has never become a real player in the game of capitalism.

To-date, the continent's resources have been effectively integrated into the global economic system. The rightful inhabitants have been left out in the cold (or at best being used as pawns in the chess game of capitalism) without being transformed into effective capitalists (Marui, 1986). This partly explains why post-independence African governments' capacity to run the inherited colonial institutions and to manage the Western production model seems to be running out of steam, and declining into decay. Look at Zimbabwe today, nothing is positive and signs of improving the current situation are almost negligible.

The Western development model has also established some form of ecological apartheid that has distanced Africans from nature. The creation of game reserves and National

Parks exclusively for wild animals at the expense of human beings, who were unceremoniously evicted from the areas with their domesticated animals, has contributed to overgrazing and conflict between wildlife service and the marginalized pastoralists living in the surrounding areas. Wild animals have not only become rivals to the domesticated livestock for grazing resources, but wildlife is in general favored over human beings and their livestock in these areas.

Paradoxically, while local people are being kept out of the parks in the name of protecting and conserving wildlife, heavy traffic carrying tourists causes noise pollution, which deliberately interferes with the wildlife breeding cycles. Sensitive animals like lions are going into hiding. Garbage left by tourists on the other hand is killing animals that swallow them largely due to obstruction on their digestion tracts. To make matters worse, poachers have turned game warders 'resulting in fluctuation between nature conservation and racketeering in trophies.

Therefore, though it can be appreciated that wildlife conservation measures and Western development culture have enhanced foreign exchange earnings from tourism and greater appreciation of the beauty of African's natural heritage; its technologies and capitalist greed have sharpened people's capacity to destroy wildlife.

For example, in 1991 it was reported that out of a population of 6 000 elephants in Uganda's National Parks in 1969, only 17 survived the attacks from armed poachers seeking ivory (EAEN, 1991). Zimbabwe and South Africa are currently facing serious poaching problems by armed men. Efforts to deal with this problem have not produced the desired results. Elephants and Rhinos are now among the endangered species of wildlife in many African countries due to poaching.

The establishment of forest plantations to supply timber to the industries of the North and to protect hillsides and the displacement of peasants from fertile lowlands by large-scale agribusinesses, all provide another good example of the unsustainability of the Western development model. Under traditional indigenous agriculture, trees were kept among other purposes, on established farmland to maintain soil fertility and their products such as fruits, timber, medicine to mention only these few.

In contrast, colonial and post-independence forest policy laid emphasis on conservation of forest for commercial purposes. In fact, by the end of the nineteenth century, forest plantations had become the dominant objective of agroforestry to supply timber. As early as 1887 (Haileg, 1957), the system which had started in 1806 in Burma, then part of the British Empire, had been introduced in South Africa. Between the period 1956 and the mid-1970s, the system was designed and implemented solely for the foresters' objectives (King, 1987).

Local farmers were exploited in pursuit of the goal of establishing cheap forest plantations (King, 1968) and large-scale agribusinesses. It was often stated that the socio-economic conditions that were necessary for the successful initiation of the system were land hunger, unemployment and a standard of living, which was low enough to border on poverty! It was the policy of most forestry administrations to remove farmers from the forest estate as soon as they got in.

The problems of man-induced soil erosion did not loom large in the thought processes of those tropical foresters who were involved with the system (King, 1987). King further states that it was perceived that the threat to the forest estate came mainly from peasants, particularly those who practiced shifting cultivation.

This was the ruling philosophy of development at that time. Foresters never envisaged agroforestry systems as being capable of making any significant contribution to agricultural development, nor did they imagine it to become a land-management system of critical importance. Yet if they had cared to exchange views with our ancestors, they would have seen the fundamental flaw in their school of thought.

The North plundered the fertile agricultural lands of Africa for more than 150 years with monoculture arable cropping, and various plantations by multinational companies from the West. Ironically, the blame for worsening food shortages in Africa, the spreading of ecological degradation and the energy crisis, are being heaped on the victims of such unsustainable development policies that were in imposed on them.

There is a re-awakening of interests in both intercropping and mixed farming, as well as agroforestry as sustainable systems of land management and for increasing productivity in the face of present land degradation. This clearly shows that these modified traditional systems of agriculture which were rejected by colonial administrators, have all along been the basis of sustainable agriculture in Africa.

The West is now realizing the flaw in its past development policies and aid support for the Less Economically Developed Countries (LEDCs). It is admitting that these policies are largely responsible for the environmental and developmental crisis in Africa and other Less Economically Developed Countries (LEDCs).

Serious doubts about the relevance of Western development policies were first expressed in the early 1970s. The Food and Agriculture Organization (FAO) and Robert McNamara, the then president of the World Bank called for re-assessment of the development policies that were made earlier pertaining to forestry and the establishment by the International Development Research Centre (IDRC), of a project for the identification of tropical forestry research priorities in the same period. That was a clear realization that earlier forestry policies were very unsustainable.

The truth is that our rural people are not naive nor naturally poor. Their current predicament and poverty is the product of having been muzzled by unsustainable development strategies imposed on them. The fallacies of the top-bottom approach hinge on the fact that rural people are considered to be naive and naturally poor. In Zimbabwe, we have what are called, 'D.D.F. roads' and 'D.D.F. boreholes' because of the top-bottom approach.

'D.D.F.' is an acronym that stands for District Development Fund, which is a development arm in the Ministry of Local Government. Non-Governmental Organizations also come to Africa with their own projects, which they impose, on local communities. This is why most of the NGOs' projects are never sustainable in most African countries, because the local communities do not 'own' them. 'Needs Assessment' or 'Baseline Survey' is key to any sustainable development.

Westoby (1975) aptly expressed the situation: *"Because nearly all the forest and the forest industry development, which has taken place in the under-developed world over the last decades has been externally oriented. . .the basic forest products needs of the people of the under-developed world are further from being satisfied than ever. . ."*

Just because the principal pre-occupation of the forest services in the developing world has been to help promote commercial forest industry development, the much more important role, which forestry could play in supporting agriculture and raising rural welfare has been either badly neglected or completely ignored.

By 1974, it had become clear to the FAO Assistant Director General, responsible for forestry that although there had been some notable short-term successes, there also had been serious areas of failure. Hence, the FAO re-directed its thrust and assistance in the direction of the rural muzzled, by laying emphasis on the importance of the forestry for rural development (King, 1979).

This U-turn to the principles embodied in traditional agricultural practices was indeed an acknowledgment of the wisdom and experience of our ancestors, which the European colonizers had brushed aside as 'primitive'. This in any way could be viewed as a form of self-confession for the environmental crisis, which had been precipitated by erroneous European policies. John Bene and his colleagues aptly and bluntly stated the confession in a report:

"It is clear that the tremendous possibilities of the production systems involving some combination of trees with agricultural crops are widely recognized and that research aimed at developing the potential of such systems is planned or exists in a number of scattered trees in different areas. Equally evident is the inadequacy of the present effort to improve the lot of the tropical forest dwellers by such means."

"A new front can and should be opened in the war against hunger, inadequate shelter and environmental degradation. This war can be fought with weapons that have been in the arsenal of rural people since time immemorial, and no radical change in their life style is required. . ." (Bene et al. 1977). King (1987), in his article on agroforestry, concluded by stating, *"Indeed, agroforestry is fast becoming recognized as a system which is capable of yielding, both wood and food and at the same time conserving and rehabilitating ecosystems."*

This recognition of the traditional agricultural practices by some scientists and institutions from the West is a step in the right direction. The 'rediscovery' that intercropping and agroforestry, which indigenous people had practiced since time immemorial were and continue to be superior to monoculture agriculture, which was introduced by the colonialists, is a credit to Africans. The new perceptions should usher in the congruence of Africa and the North of concepts, institutional change; in the design and production of technologies which reflect people's cultures, traditions and their environment.

The perceptions of the principal decision-makers and the influence, and attitude of the implementers of environment and development policies play a key role in shaping the results. In colonial Africa, there were differences in perceptions between the planners and the planned for. The failure by colonial administrators to bridge the gap, and this gulf of perceptions was a major contributory factor to the failure of many projects and to the destruction of the African environment and cultures.

All too often, there was confusion on the causes, and effects and in the interpretation of social factors. This confounded those attempting to introduce change and modernization in the continent, in particular, the rural areas. More than 70 % of the African population lives in the rural areas and yet these are the least developed. There was the ill-conceived supreme self-confidence by the colonialists who believed that the 'uncivilized' Africans could be jerked into modernity by their bootstraps using the impetus of Western technologies and cultures.

Naturally, what has happened in Africa is that either 'innovations' or interventions brought forth unsustainable development, or they have engendered much unexpected negative results. One of the major environmental tragedies in Africa, which was brought about by wrong colonial development policies and strategies, is what today is known as the 'overgrazing syndrome'. Because of the deliberate failure of colonial administrators to grasp the socio-economic and cultural organizations of the African people, they seized and gave away large areas of agricultural lands to European settlers or multi-national companies, and curbed large chunks of essential grazing lands into game reserves and National Parks.

To make matters worse, the administrators promoted the introduction and use of Western technologies in ecosystems they least understood. The consequences of these moves and development policies were that many Africans became landless. The liberation wars in many African countries were fought over land. The allocation of grazing reserves in the pastoral rangelands for other uses ignited not only the long process of environmental degradation we witness today, but also sparked off a phenomenon of hostility, distrust and violence towards colonial administrations in different countries in Africa.

When it became clear that the pastoralists and peasants were rapidly destroying their basis of existence, the explanation was tragically simple: *"The Africans were just set against change, irrational and victims of their own traditions!"* In the case of pastoralists, the colonial administrations did not want to admit that their arbitrary allocation of land, coupled with isolated provision of animal disease control and water facilities, without thorough understanding of the fragile ecosystems and analysis of the social system were the main causes of environmental destruction.

The reduction in the size of the grazing lands and the concomitant rapid increase in livestock population due to better disease control caused overgrazing which in turn encouraged soil erosion and desertification. The colonialists did not know or appreciate that wrong developmental policies and strategies had shattered the traditional ecological relationship between human beings and nature.

To turn around and heap blame on the people of Africa under such circumstances is itself irrational, unless an alternative form of security, which they could comprehend as being an acceptable substitute for their traditional proven survival strategies, was offered to them. The next chapter shows that the unfair international economic order, contradictions in vision and practices of independent African governments has aggravated the colonial legacy.

CHAPTER TWO

THE INTERNATIONAL AND CONTINENTAL SCENARIOS

"But if we do not reform, there is doubt as to whether our planetary biosphere can support economic conditions as we know them."

-Tolba, 1991

2.1 The Northern Perspective – Setting the Tune

The historical truth is that the present world economic order was both structurally and institutionally designed by the North to benefit itself. The international financial institutions like the World Bank and the International Monetary Fund (IMF) are the brainchild of the Bretton Woods conference 1944 – 1945. They coordinate international development aid; they also have the primary responsibility to serve the interests of the rich Western nations. They do not owe their existence to Africa and the institutions are there to make money for the Western industrialized countries.

In 1988 for example, the Third World countries, now the Less Economically Developed Countries (LEDCs), made a net transfer of more than US$44 billion to creditors in the industrialized West through the World Bank and IMF. At the same time, the commodity prices of goods from the developing countries took a nosedive; thereby, reducing foreign exchange earnings. Meantime; however, prices of imports from the West escalated to new levels, thus, adversely affecting the balance of payment positions of most Less Economically Developed Countries (LEDCs) and Africa in particular.

A close look at Africa today reveals that over 80% of its debts are due to borrowing from the World Bank, IMF and Commercial bilateral arrangements with the West. On a continental scale, the economic conditions of Africa itself are very worrying. Up to now, the continent still relies on producing what it does not consume and consumes what it does not control its manufacture. Agriculturally, many African countries still rely on the production of cash crops such as tea, coffee, tobacco, cocoa and a few other commodities dependent on the vagaries of nature, particularly the weather.

The fact that multi-national companies with their headquarters in the West have full control over the pricing of these products, which in any case are considered as elements of 'incidental consumption' in the North, is yet another tragedy for Africa. The North determines both the pricing of raw materials from Africa and processed goods from the North.

Because of the changed lifestyles of most African people, and the wholesale perpetuation of the Western development model, the continent imports the fundamentals of its existence, ranging from basic equipment, to food aid, advanced technologies and in some extreme cases water.

Most cars used by Africans are imported, which is a further challenge because spare parts for these cars have also to be imported, in some cases using borrowed money. Consumerism has gained an unprecedented momentum; hence, the tune has been set for Africa.
Today, Africa is more marginalized in international trade than ever before. Yet despite this fact, many African governments are not sensitizing their people adequately on the pending collapse of their continent and the need for new alternatives for survival. No meaningful initiatives are being taken to effect changes in attitudes and lifestyles of the youth to prepare them for the hard times ahead.

Bond notes (the current Zimbabwean currency), and giving the youths and civil servants residential stands in Zimbabwe are a good example. How can a young man without a job and a bank account build a house? This is living in a fool's paradise. All evidence points to hard times ahead. Many African governments stop at political pronouncements and piece-meal, water-down legislations that are very poorly implemented.

The prediction is that if no serious international initiatives towards debt resolution and corruption are taken before the end of this year (2020), the total African debt will reach a staggering US$900 billion. If that happens, it is estimated that on average, 77% of Africa's export earnings will be needed to pay the interest on the cumulative debt. For some individual countries, they will have to pay more than 100% of their total export earnings to service the debt. Some countries have reached the stage already.

How can a continent under such debt crisis and unfair international terms of trade, be in a position to implement the international environmental conventions and protocols, let alone its own environmental programme of action? Take the case of Tanzania, in 1992 it was reported to be faced with a per capita income of only US$120 a year, a US$1.5 billion import bill which was three times the amount of the export revenue and consequently forced to accept Western handouts to the tune of US$900 million a year (that was then 60% of the government's budget) to bridge the gap (Longhran, 1992).

How did the North expect such a country to implement its national environment and sustainable development as well as the international environmental conventions and protocols without meaningful global alliance? There were at that time and now many African countries that are worse than Tanzania. I must hasten to add that the situation in

Tanzania today is much better although much more is still to be done. The efforts to improve the situation by Tanzania are highly commendable and should be emulated by other African countries.

If such is the grim financial position of many African countries, then one has to ask, does the IMF and the World Bank prescriptions for economic reform actually work in Africa? Many policy-makers seem to take the IMF's central role in guiding economic reform, largely for granted and dance to the tune set by this institution, and its sister: the World Bank, only to be sandwiched between the aspirations of their people and the demands of these financial institutions.
Structural Adjustment Programmes worked out with the International Monetary Fund, which set out tough requirements for every African government such as:

- Devaluation of the local currency.
- Removal of subsidies.
- Downsizing the number of civil servants.
- Trade liberalization.
- Governance issues are no good for Africa.

These structural adjustment programmes are usually implemented without adequate preparation of the population used to government subsidies and work ethics. Consequently, even when governments put the necessary legislation in place, implementation is usually a problem or at best too slow. Mozambique had to reverse the implementation of its Structural Adjustment Programme, due to the resistance of the population, which resulted in violence, and a number of people killed.

Structural Adjustment Programmes have shown African governments that what may be a good deal and a success story in the short-term, usually turns out to be unsustainable in the long-term, because of inadequate preparation. People need to be sensitized on the implications of the IMF Structural Adjustment Programmes and indeed any programme that would affect them in the end. More often, when these programmes are introduced, people are taken by surprise, leading to resistance to change.

People always fear the unknown, which explains why they (people) resist change. The current situation in Zimbabwe that is bordering on chaos is a result of the fear of regime change from E. D. Munangagwa to someone unknown. As already mentioned above, the IMF and the World Bank were created at the Bretton Woods Conference, to run an international monetary system based on fixed exchange rates and limited capital mobility (see Michael Prowse, Daily Nation, March 10, 1992).

However, when the Bretton Woods system took on an additional role of guiding economic reform in developing countries and managing the Less Economically Developed Countries' debt crisis, it overstepped its mandate.

It is true that IMF programmes have tended to improve the balance of payments in most African countries, but its impact on inflation and living standards at best, is still uncertain. Mr. Jacque Polak, a former senior IMF official summed it this way: *"the fact that the IMF finds itself in a long term relationship of dubious value with many clients indicates something is wrong. Part of the problem lies in the mismatch between the IMF's present responsibilities and its original charter,"* (Michael Prowse, daily Nation, March 10, 1992).

Moreover, the IMF and World Bank are now admitting that they had supported some development projects in the Less Economically Developed Countries (LEDCs) that have proved to be environmental disasters. These external factors were impediments and continue to be major impediments to the establishment of sound environmental programmes and sustainable development in Africa. There is therefore a need for sharpening these capitalists' tools to see the African's perspectives and act accordingly. The major challenge is that African governments are not acting accordingly.

Of late, the West has shown some flexibility about Africa's debt crisis by writing off some debts and re-scheduling others to give temporary relief. There is still more that needs to be done! Concerted efforts and action towards resolving the debt problem and improvement in the international terms of trade would contribute to Africa's fight against environmental degradation and pollution as well as in the conservation of its unique biodiversity.

Nevertheless, Africa must know that the resolution of debt problems and international terms of trade per se will hardly solve its environmental, developmental and social crises. Africa must clean its own house. Donor fatigue has come about partly because of some serious contradictions within the African governments. These contradictions need attention now or they will come to haunt the continent forever.

2.2 The African Perspective – Dancing to the Wrong Tune

It was hoped that with the transfer of power to indigenous Africans, the ills of colonialism and the cultural barriers that had existed between policy makers, implementers and indigenous people on the other hand would disappear, and a new epoch of understanding and democracy would be ushered in. It was further hoped that this would create an enabling environment for the restoration of the African cultures and the traditional equality of sharing the gifts of nature.

Unfortunately, this has not been the case in most African countries because most independent African governments are composed of groups steeped in foreign values and with pronounced disregard for their traditions and values. In some extreme cases, some African leaders have adopted cultures that cannot be described as Western, Eastern or African.

Since most of their 'expertise' had been largely acquired in a Western or European environment and format or in developed countries, they believe it is their norms, standards and evaluation framework that apply. Thus, even where the intention on the part of the authorities is to bring benefits of modernization to the people, little, if any time is devoted to understanding their cultures and traditional ways of life.

No wonder it is only now that many African academics are beginning to appreciate breast-feeding the value of indigenous foods, farming systems and advocating for their adoption. Previously, they looked down upon these practices because Europeans had discarded them. Now Europeans have made a U-turn and they too have found it expedient to do the same.

Whilst the above factors play a role in the underdevelopment of Africa, it is however the leadership or governance that presents the greatest challenge to Africa's capacity to protect its environment, conserve its biodiversity, improve the quality of life of her people and to establish sustainable development.

The adoption of medieval monolithic mode of governance by many African leaders has caused instability in governments, encouraged ethnic and tribal conflicts, provided good ground for corruption, capital flight, civil wars, refugee problems, and leaders failing to differentiate between state and personal wealth. A case in point is the ZANU PF government in Zimbabwe, which believes that all the land belongs to it and as a result, it parcels out residential stands only to those who support the party.

The US$15 billion siphoned from Zimbabwe Consolidated Diamond Company (Pvt.) Ltd. (ZCDC), which the then president of Zimbabwe, Robert Mugabe, personally reported as missing, was also another case in point where the ZANU PF government thinks all resources belong to it. The impact of all this has been gradual institutional decay, increase in poverty, illiteracy, state terrorism, mafia-type of killing in urban centers, environmental destruction and pollution, among other evils.

Hospitals and schools in Zimbabwe have no drugs and books respectively. There is no more middle class in Zimbabwe because people are poor. Due to lack of books and poor working conditions for the teachers, there are high levels of illiteracy in Zimbabwe today. State terrorism and mafia-type of killing in urban centers are very high, also in Zimbabwe. The Itai Dzamara, Partson Dzamara, Jestina Mukoko are known cases of state terrorism and mafia-type of killing in urban centers. An 'I don't care' and 'every person for themself and God for us all' kind of attitude has been the result, making effective mobilization difficult.

Presently, ordinary people are in a dilemma as to whether European colonialists divided them more than indigenous African authorities did in the post-independence. One thing is however clear in their minds: the sentiments of oneness which colonialism had created in nationalist Africans and the traditional belonging to a community have disappeared in most African countries, and instead fragmentation and poverty are increasing.

Look at ZANU PF in Zimbabwe today, factionalism is tearing the once vibrant and revolutionary party apart. The traditional African democracy based on discussion and consensus has been stifled. Authoritarian governments have created mistrust and stress on the governed. They have in particular strained relationships among people of the same party, nation and continent. Hence, Africa now finds itself caught between the danger of anarchy (decentralized violence by the people when there is no effective government) and tyranny (state sponsored violence or terrorism designed to achieve the goal of a dictator and his cronies).

Colonization of Africans by their fellow African leaders, who yesterday cried foul play when Europeans dehumanized them, has become a more resented pill to swallow because people feel their trust has been betrayed and they have been taken for a ride. Without surprise, many Africans, some of them very highly educated and enlightened have romanticized colonialism in comparison to independent governance. Okot P'Bitek candidly illustrates the growing feeling of helplessness among Africans in his song of prisoner:

I plead sickness,
I am an orphan
I am diseased with
All the giant
Diseases of society,
Crippled by the cancer of Uhuru
Far worse than
The jaws of colonialism,
The walls of hopelessness
Surround me completely,
There are no windows
To let in the air of hope!

Today, many Africans share the sentiments of Okot P' Bitek. They blame most of the current socio-economic and political ills on post-independence administration(s). To some extent, they are right. Ethnicity and tribalism for political gain, and all their manifestations, such as religious bigotry, and nepotism are the fundamental causes of political mayhem and suffering in many African countries. They have wretched the relative ethnic and tribal calm that prevailed in the early independence era.

The widespread existence of militarism, competing with civilian supremacy has made Africa even more tyrannical and anarchist. Unless this dangerous situation is resolved, the stability and peace needed to allow people's energy to be directed to tackling their environmental and developmental problems cannot be achieved. Experience over the last four decades appears to suggest that the most important factors African governments must bring into play to promote peace, stability, unity, environmental conservation, food security and sustainable development are:

i. Equitable power sharing based on cultures and traditions of the people.
ii. Equality of job opportunities across ethnic and gender lines.
iii. Limiting of tenure of the presidency to a maximum of two five-year terms.

iv. To stop from ascending to power militarist leaders who are agents of violence, environmental destruction and underdevelopment; hence, are ill suited to govern the continent's people to greater heights of sustainability.

2.2.1 The Bully Boy Syndrome

In the light of the above scenario, we must pose a question: Can Africa's military be the guardian of environment and sustainable development as well as protect democracy? According to Bob Hitchcock, Daily Nation March 24, 1992, Africa has become notorious for security forces that wield too much power to the detriment of the national image. Repressive military regimes, which litter the continent, retard a country's development, shatter people's morale and quite often, promote crime and terrorism instead of curbing them.

The continent is tearing itself apart under militarism because state violence has bred societal violence. Merchants of death are usually armed to the teeth and believe in Maoist contention that power comes from the barrel of the gun and not from the ballot box. This is the cause of the persistent tension between soldiers, politicians and civilians on the other hand. Their pre-occupation is how to hold on to power and not how to serve the people.

The brutal behavior of Africa's militarists, which is a legacy of the Cold War strategies between the West and the East, has contributed directly and indirectly to environmental destruction, pollution, biodiversity loss and worsened the already unsustainable development.

Whenever the military stage a coup d'état or when the armed forces are used in ethnic conflict or civil war, the direct effect, include the destruction of human and animal life, destruction of properties and facilities, destruction of vegetation and large refugee influx. Indirect impacts include death due to famine and diseases, overcrowding in 'safe havens', overgrazing, environmental pollution due to poor sanitation and deforestation of areas where refugees with their livestock are camped.

Thus when the U.S. Assistant Secretary of state for African Affairs, Herman Cohen talks about African militaries having the responsibility to protect democracy, let us be very clear about the type of militaries we have in mind. Certainly, everything must be done by Africa to rid itself of the bullyboy syndrome, which has made some dictators build anti-civilian armies ranging from 100,000 to 250,000 soldiers using international and bilateral aid meant for development projects.

The armies which have in many countries maimed, killed, intimidated, put in prison hundreds of thousands of African lives, while they have displaced others both internally and externally are a liability to mother Africa. The litany of their misdeeds on the continent, are well known.

Africa requires armies that during peace times help the nation to reconstruct its infrastructure, protect its resources, and help civilians in times of natural disasters and other emergencies. In short, armies by their training have no business running a country; theirs is to provide protection to the nation and its people.

Charles Snyder, a former infantry trainer and chief political military advisor in the State Department's Africa Bureau said, *"Only after African armed forces are converted from being "Praetorian" to "Constitutional" guards who protect the constitution and territory of the nation can we regard them as defenders of democracy.*" Defending democracy leads to defending the environment, biodiversity and sustainable development for

these can only be done when there is peace, stability and individual creativity in a free society.
As of now, the purpose of most African armed forces is to defend despotic leaders, both military and other against internal rebellion. In some countries, they are used to force people to vote for the ruling parties. They do nothing beyond that! They are like the Praetorian guards who protected the Emperors of the ancient Rome.

Snyder emphasizes that a professional army in any democracy protects the institution and territory of the nation, not just an individual leader, their cronies and property (Fisher-Thompson, Daily Nation January 10, 1992). Democracy depends on an army that respects human rights, the rule of law, and the democratic system and promotes socio-economic development for all.

Therefore, if Africa is to improve the quality of life of its people, protect its environment and biodiversity, and establish sustainable development, then the first step is to have armed forces that are NOT technicians of violence. Look at violence in Chad, Mozambique, Burundi, Somalia, the Sudan, and Zimbabwe to mention just a few. The impact of this violence in terms of losses of human life, destruction of the environment and pollution is a great shame to Africa.

The continent cannot continue to create and perpetuate chaos and instability and heap all the blame for its marginalization on the West. It must accept its share of the blame.

2.2.2 Long-term Effects of African Conflicts and Civil Wars

With the exception of a handful of relatively stable countries, the majority of the African countries today are either engaged in civil conflicts and wars or are in the threshold of civil conflicts, and wars due to internal political contradictions fueled by external forces.

The militarized conflicts have resulted in large numbers of refugees, crisscrossing from one country to another causing destruction to the environment and posing food security problems. Somalia, Sudan, Chad, Burundi, Mozambique and Zimbabwe are cases in point. Professor Ali Mazrui once said, *"In Africa, power lies not in controlling the means of production but in controlling the power of the means of destruction,"* (Mazrui, 1986). What is happening in most African countries today proves him right.

With the political and institutional order collapsing in a number of African countries, many governments are pre-occupied in resisting change, resorting to management by crisis and using repressive state apparatus for social control for their survival. Under such circumstances, environmental protection and sustainable development cannot be on any priority list.

In fact, today, many governments have become the pillars of environmental and human destruction because they have abandoned their role as the facilitators of improved standards of living, social order and promotion of sustainable development. In this context, unless African governments stop the violence culture in the name of 'defending national security' they cannot be reliable instruments for enforcing environmental laws and promoting sustainable development.

A number of African governments today spend an excess of 30-40 percent of their budgets in foreign exchange buying military hardware and training repressive state apparatus with very little money allocated for environmental protection, schools, hospitals and sustainable development.

The self-perpetuating insecurity caused by the rivalry between the civilian elite and the military for the control of state power cannot allow sustainable development to thrive, let alone to be initiated. It becomes even worse when a coup d'état suddenly transforms a group of ill-equipped young soldiers into leaders of governments in the complex world. Remember Thomas Sankara of Burkina Faso in August 1983. Because of administrative inexperience coupled with half-hearted commitment to political leadership, a country becomes a land of opportunity for quick moneymaking by aliens in the confusion, at the expense of millions of citizens and environmental protection.

2.2.3 The Fallacies of the Top-Bottom Approach – The

Colonial Legacy

Many well intended economic and human resource development projects have gone to waste in Africa because of wrong perceptions, assumptions, and presumptions in their planning and implementation phases. The colonial masters in dealing with Africans adopted the top-bottom approach. It was an erroneous, but a deliberate misconception, that economic and human resources development could only be brought about by rejecting

African indigenous traditional institutions, knowledge, experience and culture.

This was so, because everything African was perceived as backward, uncivilized and primitive. Paradoxically, African elites and indigenous governments, that should know better, have furthered such convictions by their failure to modify institutions inherited at independence to suit the reality of the African situations and cultures.

Because of this attitude, there has been little attempt or effort to develop an alternative socio-political system and mechanisms based on African cultural settings to promote participatory economic and human resources development. The belief that the inherited colonial institutions were capable of promoting rapid economic and human resources development encouraged raw directives from the top to be handed out to the grass-root people in total disregard of their knowledge, experience, cultural values and socio-political institutions.

As a result, a gulf of perceptions, and mistrust between the administrators and the people have often led to failure of projects because of a silent resistance. Moreover, so goes the Third World joke: *"people pretend to work and the government pretends to pay them."* The following phrase should be added to this joke, "and both consume conspicuously above their means at the expense of the majority of the people and their country at large." This syndrome of the African governments based on acquired style of running state administration is the architect of corruption and dishonesty in the excessively state-controlled economy.

Ironically, the excessive state control is itself, a colonial legacy, which in the colonial days was designed to stifle local initiatives—a phenomenon that should have been addressed immediately after the attainment of independence. Consequently, at the national and local levels, there has never been meaningful interdependence between the governors and the governed, while at the international level, Africa has been exploited and marginalized with the grass-root bearing the brunt.

2.2.4 The Impact of Arbitrarily Fixed National and Regional Boundaries

The wholesale adoption of the colonial arbitrarily fixed national, regional and district boundaries, by most African governments coupled with the ethnic based type of administration, fragmented nationalities between and within new states. This has been another source of impediment to the development of the economy and human resources, because it has promoted nepotism, money adoration by the revelers in power and privileged positions. These in turn have caused ethnic, tribal and language conflicts, and created communication barriers due to mistrust and hegemonic tendencies.

The net result is that today, the only way national sovereignty can be maintained is through excessive use of suppressive state machinery and militarization of the political economy of the nation with exclusive right to coerce, subjugate and integrate peoples into oppressive socio-economic systems, which kill individual creativity. African leaders should now learn from the bitter lesson that forming a national government with tribal or ethnic teams will always work against the evolution of a national spirit.

Difficulties in future implementation of action-programmes intended to improve the environment and promote sustainable development in Africa must be analyzed against the impact of these negative factors. By forcing the grass-root people to improve the environment through commitment to alien models that had been a source of domination and exploitation without relating to their culture, experience, and indigenous socio-political institutions just for short-term gains is self-defeating.

It is inconceivable that governments with large proportions of their populations mistrusting one another and living in absolute poverty are going to be able to successfully demand sacrifices from such populations for the sake of environmental protection and sustainable development, the benefits of which will not accrue to them.

A critical look at the factors that have contributed to the current environmental degradation and pollution reveals that these often-ignored problems must be overcome, if sustainability, environmental protection and conservation of Africa's natural heritage are to be realized. There is an urgent need to embark on a holistic approach to address and redress the root cause of the current environmental crisis sweeping the African continent.

African culture, political and religious theology initiatives, and development concepts had been neglected or relegated to the dustbin of history, in preference for a wholesale Western model that is unsustainable in the African context. Indigenous knowledge and wisdom in resource management is vital in promoting sustainable development.

Professor Ali Mazrui (1986) when analyzing the root problem of the African underdevelopment crisis and socio-political turbulence recognized this hard-fact when he asserted that: *"A more systematic investigation into cultural pre-conditions of the success of each project, of each piece of legislation, of each system of government is required."* He went further and said, *"Feasibility studies should be much more sensitive to the issue of cultural feasibility than has been the case in the past."*

His assertion is most relevant today when there are changing perceptions of the definition of development that incorporates some general principles necessary for integrating environmental protection into the development strategies and programmes.

To translate the changing perceptions into actions, Africa needs to revisit her model of development, derived from Western ideals, culture and knowledge of complex systems. It is apparent; the application of theories based upon the desire to imitate Western achievements without adequate synthesis of our cultural, and financial constraints has contributed to our underdevelopment, marginalization, the destruction and pollution of our environment.

The current development model has proved incapable of sustaining the fragile environment, indigenous socio-economic and political structures. It also lacks the capacity to maintain links with developed industrial countries, in technology cooperation required to liberate the masses from poverty, ignorance, dependence and disease. "There is no poverty of effort in Africa; however, there is a poverty of opportunity (Somavia In Our Common Interest, 2005).

A new coherent alternative development model rooted in African culture that can promote effective environmental programmes of action, positive social transformation, and participatory institutions, is urgently required to correct and reverse environmental degradation and pollution, and to restore lost biodiversity.

Demilitarized options and community based security programmes must be part of the environmental protection programmes of action. The culture of greed for wealth and extravagant lifestyles, which are anti-traditional African values, should be shunned at all costs, if our fragile ecosystems are to be protected.

Class, race and gender-based power relations that are being lauded today are not in themselves the root cause of the problems as we are being made to believe. It is their manipulation and politicization within a given social order for selfish ends that have been the problem. The inherited power relations, and economic property that underpin the present class, and gender consciousness of superiority or inferiority complex and lifestyles are the products of that manipulation and politicization.

2.2.5 The Africa's Elites and Capital Flight

Although Africa's ecological factors and the political economy of imperialism have been central impediments to the development of Africa's capitalism, their negative effects have been compounded by ill-conceived post-independence solutions, lifestyles, and illegal flight of capital from the continent.

The sad truth is that the international unscrupulous business people in connivance with the continent's elites have illegally siphoned huge amounts of money out of Africa through various means. The indigenous shylocks have ignored the plight of the majority of their fellow Africans who are already marginalized by the political economy of imperialism. For the international business shylocks, it is understandable because they have all along been the central tools for Africa's capital underdevelopment.

They have little to lose, and care less if Africa is sucked dry and drops dead. Cases in point are the Lebanese in Sierra Leone and the Chinese in Zimbabwe. Africa's demise from the global business map would in any case hardly be felt in their countries since the continent currently represents only 4% of annual world trade volume.

The fact that many are now abandoning Africa and moving their investments to Eastern Europe and Asia is a living testimony. However, for the Africans, such behavior is a real contradiction to Africa's quest for collective self-reliance. It is a manifestation of lack of confidence in the continent, engagement in cultural surrender and acceptance of dependency on external forces. Indeed this unbecoming conduct by the local elite or petty bourgeoisie together with their propensity for luxurious consumption and for capital intensive projects, have consolidated the stage for Africa's economic dependency and vulnerability.

These people fear the implications of the single European market. They are happy to see the United Kingdom moving out of the European Union. This fear arises out of their dependency on some of the members of the European community for bilateral and multi-lateral trade ties, aid and kickbacks. Crying for sympathy will not work. They should have known better. African elites should recognize two things:

a) That the principal concern of sustainability is with the disadvantaged rural people, slum dwellers and middle class. These people must be allowed to initiate and manage their development process by providing them with facilities and equitable access to financial resources to support their grass-root activities.

b) That the demand for reform in the International Economic Order must be linked with fundamental change in conditions in Africa. That means justice, democracy, commitment and sustainability.

Justice demands equitable access to resources by the people of Africa and the return of capital siphoned out of the continent into Northern banks. The capital is needed for investment in the continent so that it fulfils the development task for which it was intended. Indigenous land rights should also be respected through comprehensive formulation and effective implementation of programmes of land tenure reform. Democracy means allowing people to become active participants in planning, decision-making and implementation of projects that affect their lives. Briefly, this means that people must become the controllers and not victims of the development process.

Desirous of compensating for the colonial neglect of the continent, and mesmerized by Western capitalism and lifestyles, post-independence African governments have been fascinated by gigantic capital intensive projects and high-tech industries such as Sheraton Hotels, huge National Stadiums, air buses and Boeing 647s, to mention these few. Appropriate and process-oriented models have been neglected. In the process, another dependency has been created: spare parts for maintaining high-tech capital equipment and machinery have to be imported from time-to-time using additional borrowed money.

In this context, the crucial question is, "does the recent fear of neglect of the continent by the West due to its shift of attention to Eastern Europe as expressed by many African governments, African Union (A.U) and technocrats a reflection of the depth of our dependency or is it a genuine concern?" To me, it could reflect both, with dependency tilting the balance. In the past, many African leaders who were patronized by the West rested on their laurels squandering borrowed money as if the international financial tap would not run dry one day.

The time has now come for African governments to face reality. Zimbabwe is a case in point. The Zimbabwean dollar was discarded in 2009 and was replaced by multi-currency, which has also failed due to externalization of funds, particularly the U.S. dollar. The country introduced bond notes in November 2016 to ease the cash shortage, but these have also not helped. The real issues are not the ones being addressed. Only the symptoms are the ones being addressed.

The greater attention to Eastern Europe may after-all, be a necessary stimulus for Africa's self-criticism and examination of its past to enable it to chart a new course that will promote collective self-reliance, and the building of African capitalism based on sustainable development and preservation of its biodiversity.

If we define culture as *"a system of interrelated values, active enough to influence and condition perception, judgement, communication and behavior in a given society,"* (Mazrui, 1986 p239), then this is the time to restore our traditional cultural values and build them into a new truly African capitalism within the continent's ecological limitation. Doing this, may usher in a new era that will allow Africans to correct internal contradictions and stop dancing to the wrong tune of Westernism or Easternism.

The shift by the West to Eastern Europe could also mean the weakening of the existing linkages of dependency between Africa and the West. It also has the potential to trigger off inward-oriented economic development especially if governments turn to their people and tap their talents.

Africa has to be aware that there was a conspiracy to keep it underdeveloped through the application of what American politicians call, "low-intensity conflict" (LIC), David Wise calls it "dirty tricks" and "covert operations" while Mkangi terms it "financial low-intensity conflict" (FLIC). This scheme has sapped the continent's capacity to develop and tightened the dependency syndrome. However, in this knowledge, the shift could be a mixed blessing.

So why cry for sympathy? Africa should instead cry for its unity and focus its attention to inter-African trade and the development of stronger economic and political ties, and blocks. This will give the continent a better bargaining power in world trade and in environmental policies. Today, it is much easier for a white person to travel from one African country to another than it is for an African. Under such circumstances, it is very difficult for good and easier trade relations among African countries. This needs immediate attention and correction!

2.2.6 The African Economic Community (AEC)

The treaty signed by Heads of State and governments in Abuja, Nigeria in 1991 to establish the African Economic Community (AEC) was a step in the right direction. However, to date, its aims and objectives are in the dustbin of history. It was hoped at the time that this would open up a new chapter in environment and sustainable development. Nothing tangible was achieved. Even the regional economic blocks such as the Southern African Development Community (SADC), Economic Community of West African States (ECOWAS), Common Market for Eastern and Southern Africa (COMESA) to mention only these, have not produced the results that they were mandated to achieve.

The recent history of Africa shows that many regional organizations collapsed because of ideological differences and suspicion between and amongst neighboring member states of such organizations. The end of the Cold War may have eased ideological differences somewhat, but the problem is still there. Today the escalation of ethnic conflicts, civil wars, heightened suspicion among neighbors and sheer greed makes the success of the African Common Market even more remote.

If the African Economic Community is to be established and to achieve its mandate, then there must be a fundamental change in the style of governance by African leaders. The 'new' system of governance must be based on sound African theology, which blends traditions, cultures and modern systems of administration. This is the credible option to take in order to stop ethnic conflicts, civil wars, greed for power and suspicion among member states. Without this radical change, the African Economic Community (AEC) and other new regional organizations will simply become mere talking fora just as the African Union (AU) is today. Radical reform in our value system, method of governance and practices is the only way forward.

CHAPTER THREE

THE INTERNAL

DISTORTIONS AT THE NATIONAL LEVEL

"National accounts should include a figure for the destruction of rural resources if countries are to see beyond short-term profit."

-Our Planet

3.1 The National Syndrome and Possible Solutions

The continental scenario discussed in the previous chapter has its root in the national character and conduct in individual African countries. This needs to be understood because that is where the correction of mistakes must start.

3.1.1 The Tragedy of Ethnicity, Tribalism and Racism

Biodiversity conservation should not be seen in terms of plants and animals only. It must include human beings. On the continent, people are becoming the most endangered species due to civil conflicts and wars, poverty, diseases and brain drain. Medical doctors and engineers are the people who leave their countries to seek greener pastures because they are in demand. People are therefore not at the center of environmental protection and economic growth.

The resultant lack of confidence in the continent, as shown by alarming capital flight, lack of information sharing due to fragmentation and suspicion among peoples, and states and uncontrolled population movements are all obstacles to the implementation of an integrated approach to environmental protection and sustainable development.

Very few African leaders have realized that there can be no peace and sustainable development where culturally diverse people of a nation have not evolved unity in diversity (Kizito, 1992). Only when people can live together, work together, have mutual respect for one another and speak freely to one another, can Africa hope to protect its environment and establish sustainable development. The key factors behind this apparent lack of realization are ethnic, tribal, and racial considerations in the method of governance and social relationships.

Ethnicity, tribalism and racialism have largely been responsible for the political mayhem in many African countries. Rwanda in 1994 is a case in point. They have also been responsible for economic mismanagement and failure to evolve able and committed political leadership. Repression, civil conflicts, and coups are usually inspired by ethnicity or racism rather than by ideological differences.

Having been submerged in the Western culture and values, the people in power and the elites have facilitated the culture of domination, profit-maximization oriented production and a conspicuous consumption mentality, all of which are anti-sustainable development.

The resulting inequality between the rich and the powerful on one hand, the poor and the helpless on the other has caused social upheavals and political instability. In turn, these have increased military spending to suppress the voice of the majority, using borrowed and aid money meant for development projects. How do we hope or expect to repay the borrowed money, if most of it is channeled to instruments of suppression of people's creativity?

Apart from military expenditure, many African countries measure development in terms of skyscrapers or high-rise buildings, luxury vehicles and other goods while poverty grips slum-dwellers, and the rural poor, because of misguided aping and excessive consumerism. Most African countries' capitals are teeming with luxurious cars like BMWs, Toyota Fortuners, Mercedes Benz, expensive Japanese and American cars. How can Africa launch an alternative vision of environment and sustainable development if it lacks moral leadership and continue to live in artificial paradise, which fuel contradiction in its value systems?

It is common knowledge that the continent is trapped in the culture of domination, conquest, and consumerism and capital-profit production. Our own leaders and people who should know better participate fully in perpetuating the status quo. Who is fooling who? If we know, we are the victims, losers and the marginalized because of an unequal socio-economic relationship with the West, why then do we practice the same principles on our people and plunder the little we have through living above our means, corruption and capital flight?

Does that show that we are genuine when we condemn the Northern exploitation, while doing the same to our people? Are we ready to take global responsibility seriously? It is important that we increase public awareness on the causes of the debt crisis namely, the unjust international economic system, and the contribution by internal practices both of which need correction.

Leaders and intelligentsia should have realized long ago the need for self-reliance in development strategies and should have woken up to the reality that it had always been their responsibility to meet the aspirations of their fellow citizens.

The foreigners with whom they had been working had their own selfish, but perhaps legitimate agendas. However, because policymakers, political leaders and intelligentsia were submerged in an alien cultural syndrome, they could not wake up to these facts when the financial tap was still running full. Instead, they danced to their whims, plundered the resources, alienated and impoverished the majority of their people. Therefore, if today the continent is gripped in a vicious cycle of poverty and a multiplicity of other debilitating crises it must share the blame.

Our African leaders are just waking up now when Europeans are more concerned about countries on their doorsteps and the tap of international finance capital has run dry. It is the educated people and those in positions of power whose minds were colonized and who take in uncritically the western ideological myths of modernization that have and continue to fail our people. The North has a solid financial and technological base. Africa does not, yet African leaders and elites who should have been the example for others do not live within the means of their pockets, governments and continent. African leaders should change their ways of thinking in order to bring change to the continent.

The power of transnational corporations, Northern governments, international financial institutions such the IMF, World Bank and IFC, and international trade institutions like GATT and ICO which have structured global economic systems in favor of the West, are not new to national policy-makers and economic planners.

African leaders and elites have always known that the arbitrary creation of their countries during the Berlin Conference of 1884- 1885 was not in the best interest of the African people. Why did they not see the need to restructure their administration? Why did they not wake up to the reality that after attainment of independence, their countries needed process-oriented and collective self-reliance approach in order to develop solid foundations?

If they chose to dance to the wrong tune set by the West and were submerged in its cultural syndrome, which the newly independent countries could ill afford, certainly they must accept their portion of the mistakes and take the first step to correct them before tackling the major culprits. Mere complaints of marginalization of the continent by the North will not protect our environment, natural heritage and bring about sustainable development. In fact, by adopting wealth accumulation models of the rich nations, we have put unbearable strain on the continent's natural resource carrying capacity.

3.1.2 Taking a fresh-look at the Present Economic Development Models.

The present national economic development model uses Gross Domestic Product (GDP) or Gross National Product (GNP) as indicators of economic growth and per capita income as measures of prosperity or standard of living gloss over key issues. They do not address seriously the question of income distribution and environmental impact of resources exploitation.

In the short-term, when the resources are still abundant and the level of exploitation is still low, the insidious social and ecological impact of the model is not visible, and the model appears to work. This has led to the assumption that the wealth generated by the few has a multiplier effect which spreads from the ruling elite at the economic centers down to the rural people.

However, as the exploitation of the resources intensifies, the unsustainability of the model becomes apparent. Scarcity of resources ignites social tension between the 'haves' and 'have nots', and environmental destruction and pollution assume alarming proportions. This is how the western economic development model has proved a failure in the long-term in Africa. Economic growth no longer reflects improvement in the quality of life for the majority.

Lack of confidence in the continent is another factor that policy makers must address. Many of us do not have confidence in investing in our own countries as Africans. Many choose to build or buy castles and villas in the North. Some swell their accounts in Swiss banks and in other northern banks with the money meant to develop our resources and improve the quality of life of our people. Some continue to collude with international crooks to plunder our heritage for short-term and selfish gains. If we are all neglecting and wrecking our own land, how do we expect the continent to prosper and the North to support us?

Let us first remove the log in our eyes so that we clearly see and then remove the log in the eyes of the North. That means we must have confidence in our own continent and individual countries, invest the little we have in them to improve the lives of our people. Actually, it is the same money banked abroad which is recycled back to Africa to loot the continent the more through interests on loans and experts' fees.

African countries should take a leaf from the experiences of Japan and Germany that were destroyed during World War II and today they are super powers. Through commitment, patience, hard work, enlightened socio-economic and political reforms; they borrowed money wisely and rebuilt their countries. They had faith in their countries and peoples.

Unless leaders and elites take seriously their responsibilities to rebuild their individual countries, proposals for a New International Economic Order, new alternative initiatives for sustainable development and conservation of the unique African biodiversity heritage will never be realized. People must be empowered and put at the center of environmental protection and sustainable development.

We cannot be taken seriously when we demand for qualitative change in power relationships between Africa and the North while our own leaders with power and privileges do not willingly surrender or share them for the good of their people. Instead when challenged, they are quick to use violence even on peaceful and constructive critics. Uganda and Zimbabwe are cases in point.

Look at the staggering numbers of warlords in many countries today who have contributed to the destruction of life, property, the environment, and the maiming and killing of innocent people. The same people proclaim on rooftops that they are the champions of environmental protection and sustainable development! They have made people on the continent the most endangered species.

3.1.3 The Debt Crisis and Internal Contradictions

The unjust international economic system has been blamed for the debt burden of Africa and the resultant cut in social services, as well as the decline in economic growth, and sociopolitical unrest. High interest rates, decline in export commodity prices and escalating prices of imports have been cited as the main factors increasing debt burden and causing debt spiral to continue from bad to worse. This is true. However, there are internal problems of our own making which contribute to the worsening of the situation that have to be addressed.

Among these is the monster called 10% or kickback and the under-invoicing of the price of export goods and the over-invoicing of imported goods that are the popular mechanisms of capital flight. The rush to catch up with

North both technologically and in life-styles without the establishment of a solid economic base, stifled higher educational systems, institutionalized ethic rivalry instead of complementarity, military expenditure, and borrowed ideologies and modes are all negative factors, which Africa must address.

3.1.4 The 10% Kick-back Syndrome

Many leaders and their cronies are today nicknamed 'Mr. Ten Percent' because they are notorious for asking 10% in illegitimate commissions of the total value of goods to be imported or of cost of projects before they can sign for any deal. This is part of the borrowed money meant for the development of the resources and people. Such money is usually banked in external accounts hidden from their people, but well known to the international community in the North from where the financial aid comes. Apart from loss of credibility internationally, to make up for the 10% forgone, many companies supply reconditioned machinery and equipment, poor quality goods or do shoddy jobs; thus, rendering many projects white elephants.

This is how some of the polluting technologies and environmentally disastrous projects have been imported and implemented in most African countries. International crooks have taken advantage of this weakness to rip off the continent since those in responsible positions have already been blindfolded with money. Such practices have spread from the top to the bottom and are responsible for the rampant corruption on the continent. It also explains why in many African countries, in spite of good environmental policies and laws, industrial and large-scale agribusinesses operate polluting industries with impunity.

This is milking the cow without feeding it! The net result is gradual decrease in milk yield and decline in reproductive rates. This is what the 10% and under-invoicing are doing to the continent's resources and its people. The 10% phenomenon, under-invoicing export goods and over-invoicing import goods, both directly and indirectly result in loss in foreign exchange revenue. Unfavorable international trade systems are therefore not the sole cause of Africa's trade imbalance. Some business tycoons and people in responsible positions contribute massively to the problem.

3.1.5 State University System and Future Generations.

A chronic lack of financial resources, political competitiveness, devastating bureaucratic practices and lock thinking have gripped most National State Universities in Africa over the last forty years. These have made many lecturers in these institutions, which are traditionally known as 'Ivory Towers' further removed from the problems facing their countries. Without surprise, the institutions that traditionally excelled in fundamental and applied research as well as in practical work of social relevance are in a state of crisis.

A closer look at most State Universities reveals the existence of two broad groups of dons: one group comprises of devoted individuals who are prepared to teach and carry out objective and creative research that is geared to solving problems. This group has little access to existing facilities due to lack of interest and flexibility on the part of the bureaucracies, and by non-availability of funding. The other group to use the phrases of Professor Odera Oruka: *"is often a praxis of intellectual ideologists who are persuaded or forced to support a political establishment."* The latter group comprises individuals that have opted for ideological alternative and abandoned objectivity.

Because of the existence of the two groups of dons, one also finds two academic axioms in many National State controlled Universities that run as follows: 'Publish or perish' and 'Lick the boots of the political establishment and that of the academic administration couched in the politics of the day or else perish'. Owing to frustration and changed objectivity, even the first axiom is no longer followed to the letter. Many academic dons are now forced by circumstances to go for money rather than quality research. Consequently, there is a tendency to publish inferior papers out of shoddy research not primarily to contribute to knowledge, but for promotional purposes. This academic materialism and intellectual disingenuousness must be reversed.

Today, it is a norm to find University dons doing the so-called research in areas unrelated to their fields of specialization, simply because aid money happens to be available for those project. Moreover, many have become secretive where openness is crucial for information sharing. Thus, today, it is difficult to defend academic mediocrity and political competitiveness because the writing is on the wall.

If university dons are to contribute positively to environmental protection and sustainable development, then the current constraints, the prices of which we are paying in retrogression of objective research and teaching, must be removed through a process of radial change. State

Universities need to be cleansed from the blackmailing and moral raping of the dons, and students for narrow selfish ends.

According to a recent study on Cost Effectiveness and Efficiency in African Universities, the quality of university education on the continent has been declining. Research and library units receive just under 3% of the total recurrent funds of the universities. Low level of funding to research and the poor state of research facilities and libraries coupled with low salaries to lecturers who are overworked have made African Universities no longer the 'Ivory Towers'. In fact, as Wachira Kigotho rightly summarized: *"The African Universities are on their way to becoming empty shells unless drastic remedial steps are urgently taken to reverse the economic and financial chaos,"* (Wachira Kigotho, standard April 4, 1992).

Let us hope that the Synthesis Report of the study conducted under the auspices of the African Association of Universities and released by professor D. Ekong, its then general secretary, has not just been the recommendations on how to revitalize Universities in Africa, but has been used to stimulate African governments to act in favor of Universities. In one way or another, African governments, as in other sectors have turned their backs on local talent in favor of expatriate professors some of whom have dubious qualifications. These expatriates follow their countries' aid money and are required to be apolitical or indifferent to all issues. Therefore, if in some countries there are many expatriate professors it is not a surprise.

3.1.6 Institutional Rivalry

Another frustrating factor that impedes proper implementation of environmental and sustainable development strategies is the intense rivalry between and within institutions. Rivalry among the mushrooming NGOs, between NGOs, Universities and Ministries has opened floodgates for political or selfish interventions that often explain the underlying divergence within the social movements. The net results are that these institutions have lost objectivity, productivity and the necessary complementarity. It should be realized that solutions to environmental and development issues call for multidisciplinary approaches.

With current difficulties in managing the many conflicting interests among these institutions, the serious question now being posed is: "how do we overcome fragmentation and develop broader capacity to create a greater impact on the environment and sustainable development projects?" The answer lies in establishing an alternative initiative that will promote cooperation while individual institutions maintain their areas of specialization and independence. The new alternative initiative that this book is advocating has several advantages, namely:

i) Knowledge is exchanged through information circulation.

ii) Complementary potentials are tapped.

iii) The current closed nature of groupings will be broken up and replaced by openness;

iv) The ability of individual institutions to respond to objective situations will be increased.

v) Collective self-reliance spirit will be enhanced through the exploitation of institutional specialization based on the principle that what is impossible in one area or institution can be feasible and possible in another.

3.1.7 The Abandonment of Environmentally Friendly Practices

The introduction of Western models of land use, the wholesale neglect, replacement of traditional systems, decentralization and the assimilation of the African elites into the Western life-styles have all played a part in shaping the environmental crisis in Africa. These made the traditional communal tenure and regulative cultural practices ineffective because most of the community land is now in the hands of a few rich people. Other lands have been turned into national parks and game reserves, as well as parastatal farms and ranches. The land has been turned into a marketable commodity and peasants turned into squatters. Look at the squatter camps in Harare, Zimbabwe, Nairobi, Kenya and many other African capital cities!

Thus, most of the land is not used for community sustainability but for growing cash crops such as tea, coffee, cotton, pyrethrum, tobacco, horticultural crops and others to raise money to service IMF loans. The consequences are the worsening food crises, air and water pollution, and the degradation of the environment by monoculture systems of agriculture, heavy use of inappropriate inorganic fertilizers and other chemicals, as well as overgrazing in the name of profit-making.

A case in point is the origin of squatters in Kenya and the growth of slums in Nairobi. They date back to 1902 when the white settlers grabbed large tracks of land in Kiambu, Limuru, Kikuyu, Mbagathi, and Ruiru, around Nairobi and beyond (Rev, Kobia, 1992). In Zimbabwe, the invasion of white commercial farms resulted in many farm workers being displaced and moving into urban centers where accommodation became a major problem which resulted in slum dwelling, which developed into squatter settlements. The closure of mines in South Africa and Zimbabwe also resulted into squatter settlements.

The Synnerton Plan in Kenya which advocated for certain class of people within the socio-economic fabric, to acquire land whilst others were rendered landless (Rev. Kobia, 1992), consolidated the capitalist development strategy that the British colonialist administrators had imposed earlier to alienate African rural communities from the control of their lands. The plan stated categorically that through the deliberate process *"able energetic or rich Africans would be able to acquire more land and bad or poor famers less"*. This was the beginning of creating a landed and a landless class (Rev. Kobia, 1992).

How many Africans were rich at the time, according to the capitalist system of things, to be able to buy large tracks of land? How many Africans at the time were prepared to go against their traditional cultural norms and theology regarding the use of land? There was a hidden agenda. Certainly, the Synnerton Plan was designed to benefit the white settlers and not the majority African communities. The resulting landless class: the Africans were envisaged to provide cheap labor for the rich white farmers who had already embarked on destabilizing the natural ecosystems with their alien practices and to provide labor in the towns. There were very few cities, if any at the time as Africans were prohibited by law to live in towns.

The Synnerton Plan effectively established an unjust class society where the virtues of self-esteem created the 'haves' and the 'have nots'. This laid the foundation of socioeconomic and political system where the integrity of humanism and the right of human beings to share the common heritage of nature's gift became grossly violated with impunity and with terrible environmental consequences.

In every African country, both in the colonial days and today, the landless squatters have no incentive to protect the land and its environment. Those in the urban centers who work as domestic, commercial or industrial workers receive meagre wages inadequate to cater for their needs such as good food, housing and clothing; hence, they are forced to reside in slums. These harsh conditions led to the rapid growth of the number of squatters on private and public lands, and slums around high-income residential areas, commercial and industrial centers as no provision for housing, and other facilities were made for laborers and domestic servants except in a few cases.

Paradoxically, the rich in responsible positions who claim to be environmentally conscious are actually the owners of most of the structures in the slums with inferior living conditions that are now the general phenomena of African cities and towns. The slum dwellers are, in most cases, the poor tenants. This largely explains why the slums are filthy, environmentally unhealthy, demolitions occur as and when they are in the interest of governments, or the rich owners who may decide to use the land for speculation or developments both with the aim of getting higher returns.

In Zimbabwe, the land has been used for political purposes with disastrous results. The youths have been given residential stands in towns and cities during election campaigns, which have always been taken away from them after the elections. In this context, people are not just living together with mutual social and environmental responsibilities. This colonial culture is anti-African and environmentally unfriendly. The same predicaments apply to the hawkers, squatters and rural communities.

How can this unjust relationship between the rich, and the poor within urban centers and rural communities be addressed, and redressed to ensure 'better environments and to promote sustainable development'? If Africans practice this exploitative relationship against their fellow Africans, can we have the moral cause to blame the West for exploiting Africa? That is food for thought!

The first step is to understand the dynamic spatial concentration of urban communities, where socio-economic activities and growth are inseparable variables. We should realize that both within, and between different communities there are interactions, and participation in the growth and development of a city within a given environment. Urban dwellers comprise of heterogeneous groups or communities based on socio-economic groupings. That is why urban communities can be divided into elite, middle, and low-income groups on one side and the hawkers, the unemployed laborers and peddlers most of whom are slum dwellers on the other hand.

The elite know the plight of the poor citizens because their activities are responsible for such poverty. Nevertheless, many have been de-cultured by Western ideas and lifestyles. Among them, one finds some of the most unpredictable groups whose commitment to environmental protection and sustainable development shift depending on the immediate circumstances (e.g. economic and political interests).

Linked to the elite groups, are the multinational corporations that hold the economies of African countries by the neck and are reluctant to sensitize their workers on environmental issues. Their rigid economic and labor policies coupled with backing from their home governments and their international multi-sectoral linkages leave most African governments with limited powers in controlling their operations; hence, there are lapses in enforcing laws aimed at improving human health, prevention of environmental pollution and preservation of environmental pollution, and preservation of biodiversity heritage.

These complex groups require different approaches based on discipline and commitment by African governments in law enforcement, coupled with persuasion to change attitudes and lifestyles. Moreover, in the case of multinational corporations, additional measures are needed involving pricking the public's conscience in their home countries and within the countries in Africa where they operate.

Slum dwellers, laborers, hawkers, peddlers and the unemployed whose understanding of the real causes of their poverty is often manipulated by the elite and the multinational corporations (MTC), require environmental action programmes different from those targeting the elite and the MTCs. They do not know that the causes of their poverty are the undemocratic and unjust global systems in league with their leaders and the elites that have marginalized them.

Environmental packages targeting them should therefore contain strong education components to create environmental awareness and remove misconceptions created by the rich people. The package should also address their economic plight to better their living standards, and conditions and re-organize their institutions or associations to give them the capacity to deal with environmental issues. Formation of residents' Associations to manage say, garbage collection, water provision, sewage disposal etc., would be effective in keeping pollution levels down. This requires good understanding of specific causes of urban environmental problems. Chapter 4 discusses the urban and rural environmental development crises.

3.1.8 Environmental Policy, Law and Implementation

Environmental concerns are becoming political issues in every African country. They are foremost subjects of political discussion today. Global warming and climate change have made the discussion more intense. After the United Nations Conference on Environment and Development (UNCED), it is likely that decision-makers and politicians who ignore environmental problems will risk national popularity, and ultimately public office. Already in the North, there is a sharp criticism of development aid policies that support ecologically devastating projects in the Less Economically Developed Countries (LEDCs).

For Africa to balance the utilization of its resources with nature there will be need for each individual country to enact appropriate environmental laws, and initiate effective environment management practices and implementation machinery. There is no doubt that every country in Africa recognized the importance of preserving its biological diversity a long time ago and states had promulgated laws to serve that goal.

However, the existing policies and laws are not comprehensive enough to facilitate the rational management of natural resources. They are more rule-oriented, requiring citizens to perform certain actions or observe specific prohibitions, failing which they faced punishment or penalties, (Ojwang, 1992). Zimbabwe has created a Ministry of Environment to deal with issues related to the environment.

With the exception of Namibia's constitution, which has specific provisions for an environment Ombudsman, most African constitutions seem to confer upon the state any recognizable authority on property regarding environmental conservation. The duty of this Ombudsman in Namibia is to, 'Investigate complaints concerning the over utilization of natural resources, degradation, and destruction of ecosystems, and the failure to protect the beauty and character of Namibia (Ojwang, 1992).

In Zimbabwe, it is the Environment Management Agency (EMA), which is tasked to monitor and enforce environmental policies and laws. Due to corruption and other limitations, many people in Zimbabwe have described EMA as a toothless bulldog. Much more needs to be done! The strict safe-guard of private property rights in most African constitutions, does not only limit the capacity of the state to intervene at the national level on environmental issues, but also stifle international collaboration to preserve global heritage.

Therefore, notwithstanding the wide range of environmental legislations, which have accumulated over the years, and many decades in most African countries, there is need for reviewing the present legislative status with a view to strengthening existing laws and their enforcement. To provide legal framework for the many existing policies, laws, and institutions related to environmental protection and preservation of biodiversity, as well as for natural resources management, special Acts such as those contained in Namibia's Constitution are necessary in order to provide basic environmental principles and guidelines.

It is high time African governments take bold initiatives at national levels to express their constitutional commitments to the cause of environment and sustainable development.

In doing this, they have to bear in mind that the effectiveness of such declarations will ultimately be measured by how well they are implemented. This calls for the strengthening of environmental law enforcement mechanisms, giving due consideration to setting up the following tribunals with adequate legal framework to persecute defaulters:

1. Inter-regional and National Waters Tribunal:
    - This will handle the problems of water pollution from various sources to ensure the maintenance of clean water for human beings, animals, industries and the conservation of aquatic life.
2. Inter-regional and National Air Tribunal:
    - This body will deal with complaints related to air pollution from industrial, traffic/transportation, agricultural and domestic waste disposal to ensure the maintenance of clean and fresh air.
3. Inter-regional and National Soil, Biodiversity and Germplasm Tribunal:
    - This body will monitor and deal with complaints related to biodiversity destruction and loss of germplasm to ensure effective conservation.

3.1.9 Environmental Education

After an environmental conference in Stockholm, Sweden in 1972, a number of African countries created National Environmental Secretariats to increase environmental awareness among the people. In recent years, Ministries of Environment and National Resources have also been established. In countries like Kenya, South Africa and Zimbabwe, curriculum for environmental management and practices have also been developed for Primary, Secondary and post-secondary colleges and institutions.

Notwithstanding these commendable efforts, environmental illiteracy is still widespread at grassroots, among industrial and business executives, scientists, economists, workers, accountants, policy-makers and implementers. This state of affairs underscores the failure of environmental education to integrate the underlying socio-economic causes of environmental degradation and pollution. Lack of funding, and comprehensive environmental policies and laws as well as poor enforcement machinery have further reduced the effectiveness of environmental education. To develop effective environmental education, there are key questions that must be answered:

- How do we convince rural people who depend on fuelwood as the sole source of energy to conserve trees when they are not provided with alternative cheap sources of energy that match their level of skills?
- With declining household food security, how can they appreciate environmental education when their social condition and their political participation are given low priority?
- In whose interest is wildlife conservation, for example? Is it to enrich African lives or to give animals the right to live at the expense of human beings, or is it for the sporting big game hunters?
- With humanity, especially the elites submerged in lifestyles based on avarice and profit maximization, how do we target our environmental education?
- What conditions will make human beings accept that environmental protection and biodiversity conservation have long-term benefits that outweigh short-term gains?
- Does environmental education place people at the center of environmental protection and economic growth?

The starting point should be to listen and learn from the people who are to be educated. They know what they want and what should be done. What they might not have are funds to implement their desires and the political muscle to influence events. In this way, environmental educationists will readily appreciate the existing problems and be in a position to develop effective strategies to accomplish the task.

For example, the traditional Acholi people of Uganda, the Kuku tribe of Southern Sudan and the Karanga people of Zimbabwe rarely cut tree species they knew required many years to mature. They used to cut those species with short regeneration time. Millet was never planted in fields where sorghum had previously been grown, because yields would be poor. Sorghum was never grown in the same field for more than 2-3 years, because they knew striga normally appeared after three years of successive cultivation. Certainly, these people were environmentally literate, and their traditional knowledge should not be ignored when educating them concerning better ways of protecting their environment.

The people who probably need intensive environmental education are the policy-makers, business executives, accountants, economists and the like who are steeped in the Western model of development, which holds nature in avarice and profit. These people need to be convinced on the huge costs of making wrong environmental decisions. Africa has no financial capacity to meet the costs of cleaning up polluted air, water and soil as well as that of litigation and medical costs. The continent's best hope lies in preventive measures, rather than in the current react-and-cure approach.

Environmental education should therefore create awareness and convince the real culprits of the importance of getting environmental decisions right at the outset of any project, social or economic. Environmental leadership training at all levels and environmental/ accounting are particularly relevant in this regard.

Brown (1990) summarized the fundamental flaw in the existing economic indicators this way: *"The economic indicators are flawed in a fundamental way. They do not distinguish between resource uses that sustain progress and those that undermine it."* Weakness is surfacing regarding the credibility of using the gross national product (GNP), which is the total value of all goods and services produced by a nation, as economic indicators that truly reflect sustainable income.

Based on this conventional economic indicator, an African country, which overexploits its resources, would get higher GNP in the short-run at the expense of the future than those countries that manage their resources on a long-term sustainable basis. For example, in the short-term, a country that over-cuts its forests for commercial purposes will certainly benefit in GNP, but in the long-term, it suffers because of depletion of forest resources and the resulting ecological imbalance. Policy-makers, private business executives and economists need to be educated on this matter.

Similarly, uncontrolled industrial expansion using polluting technologies, soil contamination arising from use of wrong inorganic fertilizers and seepage of toxic chemicals are not only sources of air, water and soil pollution, but pose serious health problems. Exhaust fumes, dust, and lead poisoning cause respiratory diseases and mental retardation. Awareness must be created on these issues.

People need to be educated on the key functions of the ecosystems. Accountants and economists should be encouraged to devise ways of putting price tags on them. Dr. Tolba (1991) reminded us on some of the fundamental principles of interdependence of living things in an ecosystem: *"Plants produce oxygen required by human beings and stabilize its concentration in the atmosphere while at the same time they utilize carbon dioxide, the main greenhouse gas, released during the respiration process."*

In addition, through their rooting systems, mineralization of the dead leaves and canopy, plants help the maintenance of soil fertility and protect water catchment areas against soil erosion. Therefore, loss of equilibrium in the ecosystem will mean eventual death of human beings (See Figure 1 above).

Environmental education should create an awareness that it is not enough for example, only to know the price of timber, fish, and minerals for short-term economic gains. People must know the consequences of over-logging, over-fishing and over-mining. Non-renewable resources must be protected from extinction at all costs.

While waste management in urban centers will definitely require new knowledge and a new combination of skills, and training for managers and operators, in the rural areas environmental education should lay emphasis on adaptive training to modernize the traditional approach. Since our rural people are the true custodians of Africa's natural resources and food security, environmental education should empower people to be the agents for the economic and social transformation of the continent. Empowering our own African people will certainly bring healing to the continent's fast-deteriorating environment. Popular participation should not be a mere slogan but a reality, which can be achieved by everyone, committed to the future of Africa.

The bottom line to effective environmental education management, remains the political 'will' to create an enabling environment that is conducive to the provision of basic human needs. It is that 'will' that will inspire governments and empower African people to take charge and shape their own destinies.

The tragic irony of Africa is that the continent's leaders, though fully aware of the environmental crisis, spend more resources acquiring guns and other military hardware as part of the illegal manoeuvres to retain and remain in power. In so doing, they have become the architects of environmental degradation and pollution. It is a shame that the same Africa that leads the world in biodiversity in terms of both plants, animal species and varieties is faced with a constant threat of hunger.

Unless the internal distortions in vision and practices are corrected, environmental education will not make an impact. African leaders and policy-makers must not dither. They must act now on environmental education and other issues such as corruption and governance. They must start now putting their acts together.

Humanity has been living in a grand delusion for too long. To stop the tyranny of the acquired avarice and conspicuous material consumption, environmental education must be given top priority alongside sustainable development programmes.

Concisely, environmental demands of the continent and the planet earth at large must supersede the human quest for the accumulation of wealth. Environmental leadership training at all levels, environmental journalism and environmental education through schools, colleges, universities, workshops, seminars and conferences need to be coordinated to achieve the desired goal.

CHAPTER FOUR

THE URBAN AND RURAL ENVIRONMENT AND DEVELOPMENT CRISIS

"Health safety in industries, the cost of polluting the air, water and soils…are other environmental issues that must be accounted for."

- *John Laird, 1991*

4.1 The Major Causes of Urban Environment and Development Problems

Analysis has shown that there are several causes to the environmental degradation and pollution processes of Africa's urban centers. The major ones include:

- High population growth arising from increased fertility and rural-urban migration.
- Uncontrolled industrial growth and physical expansion;
- Lack of funds and trained work force to provide the necessary goods and services.
- Inadequate decent housing and the accompanying growth of slums.
- Poverty and neglect of slum dwellers.
- Mismanagement of funds and other resources.

4.1.1 High Rate of Population Growth

High population growth in urban centers, coupled with poor planning and implementation have overstretched available facilities, originally meant for populations nearly, ten-to-twenty times smaller. Facilities such as water, housing, sewage systems, schools, hospitals, and other solid domestic waste disposal equipment and transport are as a result by far inadequate.

Neglect of rural infrastructure, and development or absence of gainful activities has made towns and cities attractive to able-bodied young rural dwellers. In their quest to enjoy better standards of living, they migrate to urban centers expecting better educational opportunities, health care, social security and better chances for earning money.

Many of these are school dropouts and college, university graduates whose expectations for Western lifestyles and values have been raised by education. Relatives working in urban centers and abroad are other sources of high expectations. However, once they arrive in urban centers, those who cannot find jobs or who get low paying jobs end up in slums; thus contributing to high population in slums that are caught up in a vicious cycle of poverty, a dehumanizing environment and environmental pollution.

The problem of creating more and better jobs in rural areas has remained largely unresolved. Governments have made efforts to address the problem of rural-urban migration by encouraging or spreading industrialization in all major towns, away from the cities. So far, these have met with little success because such measures are neither carefully studied, nor are they culturally feasible. In most cases, the projects are economically unsustainable. Zimbabwe came out with

the concept of service centers and Growth Points soon after its independence in 1980, but these never achieved their stated objectives. These were not culturally and economically feasible.
There is need for re-organization, and new initiatives in urban centers and rural areas giving due cognizance to African culture, traditions and values. This can be achieved through participatory approach, which empowers people to shape their own destinies in the urban as well as in the rural areas. In this connection, conflicts between traditional and government land tenure systems in rural areas and private land ownership in urban centers will have to be solved.

Many people own land both in the urban and rural areas, which is not fair for people who live in the rural areas. Dual ownership of land should be stopped as it leaves many rural people without land. People who do not own land they cultivate or live on can hardly be expected to invest in environmental protection and pollution control.

4.1.2 Uncontrolled Industrial Growth and Physical Expansion

Another contributing factor to environmental pollution in urban centers is the poor implementation or no implementation of Master Plans for the development of and provision of social facilities in towns and cities. Urban development experts have designated areas for industrial and commercial activities. Residential areas and the accompanying social services like health centers, education, playgrounds, recreation areas, churches, roads and other communication and telecommunication systems, are all planned-for in detail.

However, quite often, when it comes to implementation, political influence and economic interests override technical and environmental considerations. Zimbabwe is a clear case where Master Plans are no longer considered. As a result, plans and their implementation are accordingly changed or abandoned without regard to environmental and other considerations.

Furthermore, in nearly all African countries, urban planning for low-income earners and non-employed urban dwellers does not usually receive serious attention it deserves. The low-income earners and the un-employed are totally forgotten in many African countries. The slum dwellers and other low-income earners are only remembered, and given serious attention and consideration or mere promises during elections when the elite want their votes. Once they have ushered the elite into positions of power and influence, they are forgotten until the next general elections.

The owner-occupier housing allowances operated by many African governments benefit only the high and middle-income earners who can afford to service the high interest on house loans. Even where governments have constructed houses or flats for low-income earners, they are corruptibly allocated to high-income earners and to political functionaries. The ZANU PF government in Zimbabwe has been doing this for the past thirty years.

Left with no alternatives, the low-income earners turn to slum dwelling where proprietors in connivance with government and municipal officials exploit them. The unemployed resort to all manners of illegal street vending and trades, where they become the subject of constant and violent harassment by municipal authorities. Look at the running battles in Harare, Gweru and Bulawayo, all in Zimbabwe. Admittedly, the activities of these street vendors pollute and destroy the environment, but then authorities have neither provided alternative employment nor housing.

Environmental action-programmes that ignore these realities will not succeed. Government, NGOs and religious institutions must collaborate to address these root causes of environmental pollution of the slum communities. Multi-disciplinary approach is necessary with commitment to managing the economic, social, cultural and spiritual aspects of these environmental problems.

Uncontrolled industrial development has been another major source of environmental degradation, and particularly air and water pollution through the use of polluting technologies (i.e. obsolete machines and equipment, poor drainage, improper disposal). Such technologies release into the air polluting gases, fumes, dusts and chemical leakages. Also untreated sewage, other solid matter, and toxic effluent are discharged into rivers, lakes and oceans. Billowing columns of toxic gases and smoke into the atmosphere have become a common sight in many African countries.

Because of the stringent environmental laws and implementation mechanism in the North, unscrupulous multinational companies and individual industrialists have imported polluting technologies (and toxic waste) into Africa by exploiting the existing lax legal and implementation structures in most African countries. Therefore, there is an urgent need to tighten anti-pollution legislation and improve implementation mechanisms to stop the current trend of relocation of polluting industries in Africa.

4.1.3 Poverty and Growth of Slums

As already mentioned, Africa's poorest people are found in slums in urban centers and in the ecologically fragile rural areas. Due to economic injustice, these live in conditions of extreme poverty characterized by poor shelter, malnutrition, illiteracy, high disease due to poor health facilities, and parasite problems, low life expectancy and high infant mortality rates. This is despite the fact that all the raw materials that have or are developing urban centers come from rural areas. The theory of core and periphery is at play here. The rural poor will be discussed in much more detail in section 4.2 below.

The most severe poverty and environmental degradation, however, occur in urban centers where low-income earners and the unemployed are forced to live in slums located in geographically hazardous areas or too close to dangerous industries. Such areas include steep slopes, where landslides are common and valley bottoms, which are subject to periodic flooding and mudslides. This rapidly growing trend is putting massive physical environmental strain on urban centers and dwellers across Africa.

The high levels of forced environmental illiteracy among the slum dwellers, as well as low educational standards will continue to pose a myriad of urban environment problems, unless the root causes of their poverty and the resultant poor living conditions are addressed in concrete terms. Mere slogans and political statements will not help.

4.1.4 The Types of Pollution

The fore mentioned causes compounded by lack of funding, trained work force and sheer mismanagement of available funds cause air pollution, water pollution, soil contamination with severe consequences on human health, aquatic life, vegetation growth and crop production. Each of the major types of pollution is discussed below.

a) Atmospheric Pollution

Air pollution refers to the release of energy and substances into the atmosphere in quantities and durations liable to cause damage to human, plant and animal life, to manmade materials and structures. These can also result in global warming; interfere with the comfortable enjoyment of life, property or other human activities (Elson, 1987).

Today the major culprits of air pollution in African urban centers are vehicles and industries, which produce or emit toxic chemical compounds like carbon monoxide, nitrogen oxide, Sulphur dioxide, hydrocarbons, lead, chlorofluorocarbons (CFCs) dusts etc. (Obudho et.al, 1991, Oloo, 1990). The burning of charcoal, garbage, rubber and petroleum plastics follows these. Tanneries are notorious for repugnant odors in the immediate environment. These atmospheric pollutants are responsible for most respiratory diseases like silicosis, byssinosis, (Merchant, 1989, Sakari, 1989) heat island, acid rains etc. that damage vegetation, crops, structures such as buildings, clothing and aquatic life. Depletion of the ozone layer and change in climate are also caused by atmospheric pollution.

The absence of strong legislation and implementation mechanism make the observance of safety margins of air pollution difficult. As stated earlier, much of the industrial activities found in urban centers in African countries are carried out by heavy polluters who have escaped stringent pollution control laws in their own countries and who take advantage of corrupt officials and the lax legal structures.

b) Water Pollution

Water pollution in African countries comes mainly from dumping of imported and locally generated industrial wastes, sewage discharge and surface run-off water. International conspiracy to pollute African waters with toxic wastes from industrialized nations came to light in 1992 when an Italian ship loaded with toxic wastes from Europe was caught dumping such waste in West Africa. A British owned multinational company, Thor Chemicals imported toxic waste from the industrialized North and dumped it at Cato Ridge in South Africa (Daily Nation, March 13, 1992).

As if that was not enough, the World Bank Chief Economist Lawrence Summers wrote an internal and confidential memo that was equal to adding insult to injury. He said that the less populated African countries were 'underpopulated' and that any diseases caused by contaminants such as cancer would cause less economic damage in developing countries (Daily Nation and Standard, February 9, 1992).

Mr. Summers then reasoned that 'dirty' industries should simply be transferred to the poorer countries. He went further to say, *"I think the economic logic behind dumping a load of waste in the lowest-wage country is impeccable."* Can you imagine such statements coming from a senior World Bank official?

Is this not the same bank that all African Governments turn to for development aid? What do these statements mean to Africa? Moreover, why this irrational attitude and action towards Africa? Does this not complicate Africa's problems vis-à-vis her development relationship with West?

If the West is serious about the protection of the Global Environment, then the first step toward resolution of the environmental crisis is to condemn and stop these unbecoming behaviors of its citizens towards Africa. The West must take decisive measures to put a stop to these self-defeating practices. Queen Elizabeth in one of her Commonwealth Day messages once said, *"The Earth is a gift to us all, whoever we are and wherever we live. We have but one planet and all life on it is interdependent."* Her message is loud and clear to all people of good will.

Therefore, let no individuals in the West imagine that dumping wastes in Africa will make the West a safer place to live in. If Africa sinks, it will sink with the rest of the world because it is part of the same ship: planet earth. On the national front, African policy-makers and implementers must stop behaving as the proverbial ostrich that buried its head in the sand and believed it had protected itself from the gathering storm. They must take serious views and actions to reduce pollution. There is a strong feeling that insufficient action has been taken to protect the environment, in particular prevention of water pollution.

Environmentally unsound industries are being set up with approvals from authorities and industrial toxic effluent, and solid wastes are being dumped into waterways and then into rivers, lakes or sea with impunity because of some form of kickback. Untreated or semi-treated sewage is usually disposed by being discharged directly into rivers, lakes and seas with serious implications for marine and aquatic life as well as human health. Among the leading industrial consumers and polluters of water are the chemical industries, tanneries, textile mills, paper and pulp mills, steel plants and hydropower stations (Muslim, 1975).

For example in Kenya, by early 1979 Mombasa town was discharging 5.4 million liters of waste into the Indian Ocean. At present, much of the waste from Kisimu town was disposed into the Kasat River, which flows into Lake Victoria. In Kisii town, untreated sewage is discharged directly into the nearby river causing water pollution for a long distance downstream (Obudho et. al 1991). In Zimbabwe's capital city Harare, untreated sewage is discharged into the Manyami River, which flows into Lake

Chivero. As a result, most people in Harare rely on bottled water for drinking. Even borehole water is not safe as studies carried out in Harare and Bulawayo in 2014 can testify.

Storm water from urban centers carries all sorts of waste, which it finally dumps into river systems, which in turn empty them into lakes or oceans. Water pollution poses a number of problems. Through depletion of Biological Oxygen Demand (COD), it causes the death of aquatic life (West and Biney, 1991; Biney et. al. 1987, Alabaster, 1981). Provision of clean water supplies is now very difficult both for domestic and industrial use and risk of diseases like typhoid, dysentery, diarrhoea, schistomiasis and others is on the high in most African cities and towns.

c) Solid waste Disposal Problem

The management of solid wastes poses one of the greatest challenges to urban authorities in modern Africa. Rapid urban growth both in terms of physical expansion, and human population coupled with strained administrative capacities have rendered urban solid-waste management services ineffective in many cities and towns. The negative social and health effects of failure to collect garbage is felt most among the poor slum dwellers on neglected public lands.

Lack of community spirit of collective self-reliance, conspicuous consumption of the rich urban residents beehive of industrial and transport activities have accelerated the accumulation of solid wastes at alarming rates in recent years. Zimbabwe is hardest hit by the failure of local authorities and municipal councils to collect garbage, which has resulted in diseases.
The major types of solid waste generated in urban areas include household wastes, commercial refuse from stores, offices, eating houses and restaurants, hotels, warehouses, ports, refuse from institutions like schools, colleges, Universities, hospitals and transport terminals (e.g. airports, railway stations, bus and public transport stations and depots).

While managing solid waste is one of the most costly services to provide (UNCHS Habitat, 1988), urban authorities in Africa cannot be forgiven for abandoning their responsibility. The fact that household, commercial, institutional and street solid waste account for about 90% of all urban wastes in the Less Economically Developed Countries (LEDCs), (UNCHS, Habitat, 1988), is a sufficient reminder to urban authorities that they must re-think and find solutions to regular removal of these enormous wastes.

Another alternative is to change course and abandon the unsustainable lifestyles to reduce the burden. Leaving mounds of rotting waste near public buildings, near residential houses, hospitals, and industries, centers of towns and cities, and public recreational premises is a sure way of increasing health hazards and water pollution.

Whether solid waste is biodegradable or not, it must be disposed of properly, otherwise, it becomes the breeding grounds for flies, rats, cockroaches and other pests, which are disease vectors. Leachate from decomposing garbage produce repugnant odor and percolates into the soil, or the effluent flows into nearby water bodies causing contamination. When swept by surface runoff, the rotting materials block waterways, drainage channels causing flooding in cities and towns, creating stagnant water, which provides a good breeding ground for mosquitoes.

Financial constraints should not be the first excuse for failing to provide efficient garbage collection systems. Quite often, the failure to use efficiently the available resources is the major cause of inefficiency. Diversion of resources into non-priority areas, buying the wrong technology in the form of equipment and trucks due to corruption are some of the common practices that lower efficiency in rendering services.

The message to African leaders is loud and clear: firstly, Africa must use efficiently what is available to keep the environment clean before clamoring for more. Secondly, unsustainable development strategies and lifestyles, which are anti-African culture, must be abandoned. Thirdly, collective self-reliance through the formation of resident associations to give rebirth to community spirits must be encouraged. Lastly, we must go beyond materialistic and cost-oriented communities in order to achieve environmental cleanness and protection.

The choice must first be good health, through good and clean neighborliness, as well as better disposal systems; the rest will follow. Once the moral obligations of our urban societies have been restored, then curbing urban environmental problems can be possible using various technical means. Studying 'waste culture' could reveal the way forward.

4.2 The Rural Environment and Development Crisis

4.2.1 The Crisis and Resolutions

Human beings throughout history have been key players and components of the environment. Yet, during colonial and post-independence administration, governments have paid scanty attention to understanding human ecology, in particular that of the rural people, as part of the development process. Ironically, a lot of attention has been given to wildlife ecology as a basis for proper management and preservation of the African natural heritage.

According to government officials and local priests, Ugandan Pygmies face extinction today because of government neglect (Sunday Times, March 29, 1992). The Bushmen in Botswana and Zimbabwe are facing a similar fate. This is so because 'Bushmen and Pygmies are of less significance than wild animals.' A local priest reported that the pygmies were not even counted by the government of Uganda during the censuses. Paradoxically, game animals are counted at regular intervals.

Past and present neglect of the basic rules of pastoral and agro-pastoral systems had been and still are the main cause of environmental degradation and decline in animal and crop production. In extreme cases, the areas that once thrived with diverse agro-pastoral systems have become barren deserts. Former white commercial farms in Zimbabwe are a good example. Also to blame, is the lack of clear understanding of traditional values and practices by African elites educated under western models, in Western-like settings that have condemned wholesale African cultures and traditions as primitive and threatening gender superiority.

Because of the lack of appreciation of African cultures, the colonialists were frustrated and they blamed the apparent 'irrational, perverse or mystical' behavior of rural communities. Are the African elites aping the colonialists at a time when even the European scientists and lobbyists are beginning to appreciate the wisdom of traditional agricultural practices such as mixed cropping and agroforestry? If this is so, then God help Africa!

Let us research and interpret indigenous traditions and cultures with sober minds. The greatest sign of hope for Africans from the agricultural and environmental points of view is the silent grass-root revolution, taking place in villages across the continent. Millions of peasant farmers are busy organizing themselves into village self-help groups with the help of NGOs and churches.

The small-scale farmers are aware that due to wrong government development strategies and policies, they have been faced with growing challenges and difficulties, which in some areas have contributed to rapid environmental degradation and a decline in food production and standard of living. The strains have been especially immense for women and children. Today, rural women have to walk for distances ranging from 1-40 km in search of water and firewood, and more than 70 km to sell their produce (Sunday News, March 8, and Sunday Times, March 15, 1992).

Pastoralists are equally aware that they have overgrazed the rangelands, which are their basis of life support. However, they are also aware that they have no alternative because their essential grazing lands have either been curbed into game reserves or National Parks, or turned into cropping lands by governments. Hence, the pastoralists watch helplessly the destruction of the environment under the uncoordinated government development programmes.

In contrast, peasant farmers have not been passively waiting for outside aid. In the Sahel region for example, since the early 1970s, local key innovators have been organizing villagers at the grass-root to undertake a variety of developing projects. Similar initiatives have been undertaken in many other countries like Kenya, Botswana, Zimbabwe, Senegal, Burkina Faso and others.
In these countries, it is important to note that governments have acted in partnership with the rural farmers allowing them to organize themselves with little intervention, which increased their motivation.

In countries where progress has been stifled, governments have been suspicious of anything resembling nationwide farmer's organizations. Instead, governments have forced farmers into state-run cooperatives, which have proved financially and environmentally costly. Zimbabwe in the early 1980s and Tanzania earlier are good examples.

With regard to the gender question, one of the most significant features of the silent grass-root rehabilitation in agriculture and environmental protection has been the role played by rural women. In both numbers and level of active participation, women have outshone men. They are better organized, more disciplined, more dependable and hardworking.

Although there are no universal valid packages for achieving sustainable development because conditions in individual countries differ widely, the key to rural sustainable development and environment can be expressed in one word: 'empowerment'. Governments, politicians, business communities, industry and NGOs should pay attention to grass-root people who are best acquainted with local ecological, economic and socio-cultural conditions.

Through self-organization, starting at the village level, peasant farmers and pastoralists alike can master, and shape their own destinies through democratically made decisions concerning their development needs. This approach will also make them appreciate that sustainable development is a process as well as a goal, which they can slowly master. After all, their ancestors and mothers knew it, and passed their experience and wisdom to them.

Unless the local population are convinced of the advantages of improved balance resource management and deeply become more involved in the design and planning of the environment and development projects, conflict will inevitably arise between the need to protect and the need to exploit natural resources.

NGOs and religious clergy and laity who are able to draw on comprehensive specialized knowledge, innovative stimuli and personal initiative are best placed to spearhead grass-root environmental conservation and the establishment of sustainable development within governments' development and environment guidelines. Secular leaders, though may be committed to the cause of the rural poor or disadvantaged urban dwellers, often do not appeal to the minds, hearts and the souls of such communities. It is the cleric or laity oratory, based on the Bible and basic needs that usually inspire-up people especially the disadvantaged people. Their skills can be effectively employed for the cause of environmental protection and sustainable development.

4.2.2 Grass-root Communities and Biodiversity Conservation

The richest habitats for biological and genetic resources are the tropical rainforests. Of the 23 000 species of plants estimated to occur in South Africa, Lesotho, Swaziland, Namibia and Botswana, countries with a Mediterranean climate, 80 percent are endemic to the Southern African region (Tolba, 1991). Nobody knows accurately the total number of plant species in the tropical rainforests of Africa, let alone animal species.

If in only a 15-hectare area of Borneo tropical rainforests approximately 700 species of trees have been identified, then one can imagine what would be in millions of hectares in Africa's tropical rainforests. The species found in the Southern African region alone are 1.7 times those found in Brazil (Tolba, 1991).

The sad thing is that as much as 1.7 million hectares or more per year (Tolba, 1991) are reducing the tropical rainforests, the home to about 50 percent of the world's entire biodiversity. Deforestation is the immediate cause of the loss of biodiversity. However, the underlying causes are wrong development policies and plundering by local and multinational companies over the years.

Farming, particularly ranching is taking large areas of the rainforest. These have brought about inequalities in land distribution and use, and caused insecure land tenure; unsustainable commercial exploitation of the rainforests for timber; disruptive schemes such as building of hydroelectric power stations, establishment of large forest plantations and cash crop plantations.

The Tropical Rainforest Action-Plan (TRAP) designed from overseas and the National Forest Action-Plans (NFAPS), which were hailed by aid agencies as the answer to tropical rainforest's crisis, have proved unrealistic because they were all biased towards industrial forestry, involving commercial plantations meant for producing export-oriented forest products (Daily News, January 16, 2004).

The survey of the TRAP and NFAPS in the countries where the schemes were initiated indicated that such schemes were incompatible with locally based efforts towards a more democratic and social order on which the only realistic hope for saving the tropical rainforest rested. It was after the realization that the above plans were doing more damage than good that environment and development agencies turned to the grass-root people, in developing countries for solutions to the rainforest crisis.

Soil contamination caused by persistent use of wrong inorganic fertilizers in the monoculture system of agriculture is another factor. Many farmers are now complaining of the decline in cereal crop yields due to the increase in soil acidity. The monoculture system has also caused a reduction in plant and animal diversity and it has encouraged the spread of pests and diseases as well as obnoxious weeds. As a consequence of the negative effect of the introduced 'modern' farming systems, local small scale farmers are now returning to the traditional practice of organic farming.

Because of the unsuitability of the foreign development model, local communities with a wealth of knowledge and experience in their local ecological systems are finally being recognized. NGOs, religious people, government agencies should work closely with local community groups to achieve environmental protection and sustainable development.

CHAPTER FIVE

THE FRAMEWORK FOR RESOLUTION OF ENVIRONMENTAL AND DEVELOPMENT CRISES

"Decision-making is easy if there are no contradictions in your value system."

-Robert H. Schuller, 1984

5.1 The Task for African Countries

The one-sided socio-economic model of the West, which was introduced into the continent with the advent of colonialism, is largely the root cause of the alarming environmental degradation, biological diversity loss and the unsustainable development. Its continual application by indigenous governments over the years without adequate understanding of the local ecological and technical processes, and in disregard of the real aspirations and needs of the African people is a big shame to Africans. Never in the history of Africa has its peoples been under attack on so many fronts as it is today. This is a sign that we have gone too far and too fast in the wrong direction.

In the interest of future development and generations, Africa should reject the present path of resource consumption of the North. Currently, industrialized countries get more than 85% share of the world's income and consume more than 70% of its energy, 75% of its minerals, 85% of its wood and 60% of its food (UNDP, 2013). If we, as Africans, blindly continue on a similar path, we will further degrade, and pollute our environment and compound the existing socio-economic problems.

Strategies for sustainable living in Africa call for practical guidelines to the policies and laws, which must be adopted, and actions that must be taken. More importantly, they call for the 'will' at international, national and community levels to undertake the principles outlined below without reservation, and above all, with people placed at the center of environmental protection and economic growth.

a) Halt the ruthless exploitation of the continent's resources by multinational companies and greedy indigenous people.
b) Strengthen Environmental Policies, Laws and implementation machinery. In the case of Zimbabwe, the Environmental Management Agency (EMA) should be given more powers in order to have teeth.
c) Advocate for the conservation of the entire continent through networking and collective self-reliance.
d) Recognize the close relationship between nature conservation, the production of indigenous peoples and the satisfaction of their basic material needs.
e) Change indigenous personnel, and community attitudes and practices to live within the continent's capacity to support life.

f) Create an enabling environment that allows communities to care for their own environments through the formation of urban resident associations and village committees.
g) Provide national frameworks for integrating conservation with development (e.g. by establishing environmental units in Ministries, industries, local governments, and at village and community levels).
h) Respect and care for community life especially the disadvantaged groups such as the rural poor, the slum dwellers, the disabled and abandoned individuals.
i) Provide legal framework that prevents industrial pollution of air, water and land degradation (e.g. formation of African Environmental Tribunals, National Water and Air Tribunals, National Soil Conservation Tribunals etc. and incorporation of specific Acts on Environment in Constitutions).
j) Provide equal opportunities for all across ethnic, and gender lines to participate in environmental and development issues.
k) Create effective global alliances to ensure the caring of the Earth as a whole.
l) Integrate the activities of the government with those of NGOs, Religious bodies, Universities, Colleges

and Vocational training institutions in order to achieve good results through joint coordinated endeavors.

m) Incorporate African theology in environment and development issues.

n) Provide a framework for effective implementation of strategies for managing change that affect both the environment and development.

o) Establish Regional Environmental Leadership Training Centers.

5.2 Global Alliance: Is it a Myth or a Reality?

Can Africa count on a global alliance? Will international politics on the environment allow for a common stand and agreements that will ensure strict, systematic environmental impact assessments to be adhered to for the benefit of all?

Already there is a key disagreement among nations regarding the limits of carbon dioxide emissions. This all started when nations were heading for the much publicized Earth Summit in 1992. The United States, the world's largest single producer of carbon dioxide gas (CO2) was not supporting a widely accepted European Community proposal to cap CO2 emissions at the 1990 levels at the time (Sunday News,

March 22, 1992, Sunday Standard, March 29, 1992). President George W. Bush vowed at the time that he would not sign a treaty to fight global warming if it threatened American jobs. He said that his decision on whether or not to sign the treaty was going to be based upon 'the extreme need to keep the country's workforce at work and to get more people working.'

His priority seemed clear: 'to maintain the American way of life first, irrespective of global warming and its dreaded consequences'. George W. Bush has gone, but the American stance on global warming has not changed much. African leaders and policy-makers should not take a leaf from this American stance and act accordingly and appropriately.

It is now common knowledge that there is international pressure seeking to make diversity therein 'the common heritage of mankind'. Because of this, a legal binding arrangement in the form of an international convention to protect these tropical resources was drafted for the UNCED. The real reasons for the conventions were that developed countries were increasingly looking to these resources for germplasm they needed and they were aware that the tropical rainforests provided the single largest CO2 sink. As such, they were strategic and could influence global climatic change. This would bring into play international environment politics, and aid at the UNCED and beyond. Africa and the Less Economically Developed Countries (LEDCs) must be on the lookout.

Another hot issue that has become the center of the argument in recent years is about the funding of Agenda 21. Agenda 21 is a comprehensive plan of action to be taken globally, nationally and locally by organizations of the United Nations System, Governments and Major Groups such as UNICEF, UNESCO etc., in every area in which human impacts on the environment is felt. This was adopted in Rio de Janerio Brazil by more than 178 countries on June 14, 1992.

The questions asked then and continue to be asked today are: 'who will foot the bill estimated by the UNCED Secretariat then to be US$125 billion needed to implement Agenda 21, the plan of action for sustainable development? How and by whom will this money be provided?' These questions were of concern then and continue to pit the G-77 against the G-7 nations. The G-77 nations wanted and continue to demand that the North provide the money since it is made up of the world's richest and advanced nations.

The North appeared then and continues to be unwilling to foot the bill, because to raise the estimated US$125 billion it would require it to increase the current 0.35% of its GNP given in aid to G-77 to approximately 1%. Judging from the arguments advanced by the North at the drafting of the document that was prepared at Prep.Com.4 regarding the amount of the money and the mechanism for funding, it seemed clear the exact figures and dates would be omitted from the document that was to be presented to UNCED in 1992. Some members of the committee who drafted the document described it as "constructive ambiguity".

Let it be hoped that the many treaties on biodiversity and agreements on global conservation and forest management will be signed by all the G-7 countries soon and will benefit Africa as well. Moreover, let us hope that the United States of America will earnestly continue to restrain its carbon dioxide emissions and the rich North will fully fund Agenda 21. Otherwise, the future looks bleak for Africa. If Africa does not reform then humanity will have to gear up for a catastrophe. Our planetary biosphere has already sent out a warning that it can no longer continue to support economic conditions steeped in avarice and profit. Nature functions on the principles, which maintain checks, and balances to guarantee optimization and equilibrium. Africans must conform for their survival.

Jesus did warn against the Teachers of the Law and the Pharisees when he told his disciples: *"The teachers of the law and the Pharisees sit in Moses' seat. So you must be careful to do everything they tell you. But do not do what they do, for they do not practice what they preach. They tie up heavy, cumbersome loads and put them on other people's shoulders, but they themselves are not willing to lift a finger to move them. Everything they do is done for people to see . . .,"* (Matthew 23 vs. 2-5 {NIV}). Africa's hopes on the UNCED were plagued with 'The Teachers of the Law and Pharisees'. Look at Uganda, the Sudan, the Gambia, Zimbabwe, Democratic Republic of the Congo (DRC) etc. today.

5.3 African Theology and Sustainable Co-existence.

"African traditional societies are community centered, and their philosophy is based on the maintenance of a balance or equilibrium between human beings and their environment. All members of the community are expected to show a spirit of collective responsibility, mutual obligations and solidarity. . .The collective community good and sacredness of life provide the ethical foundation of human rights and respect for the environment," (SONED, 1991). *"The relationship*

between mankind and nature is basic to all African cultures and yet remains intimate," (Ali Mazrui, 1986). These quotations summarize African traditional attitudes and beliefs towards nature and its Creator.

They also emphasize the awareness of dependence on nature's gifts and the need for sustainability. African religions were in fact tailored to create this awareness and to articulate the relationship between human beings, nature and the Creator. The spirit of sustainable co-existence is therefore deeply rooted in the minds of traditional indigenous Africans. This explains the great influence of tropical ecology and climate on African traditions, cultures and technology. Traditional Africans believed that they were part of and NOT the controllers of nature; therefore, they evolved their way of life in response to the environment in which they lived.

How does the African theology of collective self-reliance, empowerment and sustainable co-existence within the community and with nature compare with Jesus Christ's model and those of Taoism and Confucianism? The Bible tells us clearly that Christ came to awaken and empower the disadvantaged people to assume fully their human quality within God's laws. He preached the values of God's

Kingdom as resting on justice, sharing, caring, rendering service to others, solidarity and ability to persevere and resist temptation. In this context, Christ concurred with the essence of African theology, traditional and cultural ideals.

Tao and Confucius were two great Chinese philosophers who lived about 551 B.C. and shaped Chinese religions and people with their thoughts. Taoism preached the idea of co-existing with nature and urged the Chinese people to return to nature. Confucianism, on the other hand, took a more pragmatic approach by teaching the principles that could maintain social order (Watch Tower Bible Tract Society, 1990). Confucius taught that everyone, from the emperor to the common folk, must learn what role he or she was expected to play in society and live accordingly.

Talking about the rule of conduct (li) and humaneness (jen) Confucius had this to say in the opening chapter of The Great Learning, *"When true knowledge is achieved, then the will becomes sincere. When the will is sincere, then the heart is set right; when the heart is set right, then the personal life is cultivated. When the personal life is cultivated, then the family life is regulated. When the family life is regulated, then the national life is orderly and when the national life is orderly, then there is peace in the world."*

Confucianism, therefore, talks about the importance of regulating one's life, peace, justice and harmony in society. Here again one sees the similarity in emphasis between Chinese and African theology. Is this common agreement about human life a coincidence?

When Jesus, through His teaching and deeds, challenged the injustices, hypocrisy, corruption, over lordship and wastefulness that is similar to today's, He was killed. However, the truth remained. Life in its fullness and sustenance is achieved only when justice is practiced, that is the only path to maintaining equality, social balance and to keep nature in equilibrium, the way God set it to work. When our ancestors resisted the theology based on conquest, greed, uncaring and of individualism, the colonialists descended on them, massacred many of them, and took live ones as slaves. However, they left behind an enduring truth that is being re-discovered today.

The theology of conquest, the Promised Land, individualism, chosen people, abundance and of laissez faire is the secular Theology of Christendom, not of Christianity as Jesus and his first disciples preached to humanity. Christendom refers to the realm of sectarian Western style

Christianity whose activity was dominated by religions that each claimed to be a Christian.

In contrast, Christianity refers to the original form of worship and access to God as taught by the words, and deeds of Jesus Christ and his first group of disciples: a theology, which agrees in principle with African theology. Christendom is the product of the waves of religious reforms and industrial revolution. This secular theology is the one that was imported to Africa by Europeans looking for freedom and wealth. This theology destroyed African traditions, value systems and cultures, plundered the resources of the continent and set not only Africa, but also the whole world in a collision course with nature.

This being the case, one may ask: "could it be that the God of Africa sent Jesus Christ to preach to the Jews about His Kingdom, which was based on justice, sharing, caring, and rendering services, solidarity and living in harmony with all His creation? Was it a coincidence that God told Joseph and Mary to take refuge in Africa?" One day the truth will come to the surface to correct history.

African leaders who stepped into the Whiteman's shoes have replicated the same theology of conquest with even greater intensity as shown by the scale of civil wars, refugees, loss of human lives, destruction of the environment, and the unjust distribution of wealth. Look at Sudan, Somalia, Burundi, Democratic Republic of Congo, Zimbabwe etc.

Jesus condemned the hypocrisy of those holding on to power when He said, *"Woe to you, teachers of the law and Pharisees, you hypocrites! You travel over land and sea to win a single convert, and when you have succeeded, you make them twice as much a child of hell as you are,"* (Matthew 23 vs. 15 {NIV}).

The task of environment and development crisis resolution in Africa must involve the application of the theology that empowers individuals and communities to conserve a balanced exploitation of natural resources, and bring about quality of life for all. It must be the theology that can be used as a tool to analyze socio-political and economic roots of the continent's problems, and help create political conditions that make ecological responsibility possible.

Certainly, the theology of Conquest, the Promised Land, abundance, the elite, and of laissez faire attitude cannot help. African Christian theology based on the synthesis of our traditional values, those Christ's teachings, and Confucianism, seem the best option for integration into the action-programme for environmental protection and sustainable development. Clergy and laity are better placed to carry out this synthesis, and the application of it to the environment and development crisis resolution.

The theological basis for such participation stems from the fact that nature, socio-economic development and the spiritual aspect of human beings are intertwined. In the book of Genesis Chapter 2 vs. 8-12, the Paradise in which God put Adam and Eve is described as a garden full of biological diversity, which exhibited perfect interdependence and functioned in accordance with God's laws.

Disobedience by Adam and Eve led to their expulsion and loss of the Paradise when they misused God's gift by eating the forbidden fruit. Modern human beings appear to be heading for a similar fate unless something drastic happens. Churches and Mosques are therefore, duty-bound to rescue humanity from the path that leads to destruction. They have a right to participate. The universe is unfolding and must be at peace with God.

5.4 Managing the Changing Perceptions

In all African urban centers, there are slums whose growth is accelerating at an alarming rate, while in the countryside there are the rural poor that are destroying their life support systems. All these problems are the products of economic suppression and marginalization to which these people have been subjected. The difficult conditions have forced these people to engage in activities that contribute to environmental degradation and pollution.

On the continental scale, governments are losing the capacity to render social services, maintain infrastructures and buildings, and in all sectors, Africa is showing signs of decay. Through this, Africans pay the price for adopting the development model of conquest domination, and ruthless exploitation of nature and people.

The changing perceptions towards the environment and development, which are sweeping the whole world and the shift of the West to Eastern Europe means that Africa, must gear itself to manage the inevitable change. The events (political, economic and social) that have been unfolding in Africa, however, indicate that the continent is not gearing itself properly for the change.

Democratic processes are being suppressed violently. The authorities and the rich individuals that should care for them are evicting the poor slum dwellers, and rural people who are the vanguard of industrial labor force and agricultural production ruthlessly. Civil wars, ethnic and racial conflicts are being instigated or intensified, where they already exist. These approaches to managing change are compounding environmental and developmental problems.

African leaders convene summits where they cry wolf and appeal to the North to come to their aid and help them clean the mess they themselves have created, a clear mockery of independence. Look at the Gambia, the Democratic Republic of the Congo and Zimbabwe etc. They must stop killing the goose that lays the golden egg.

This sad situation is illustrated below by looking at a few cases. In Zimbabwe, in the early 1980s there were conflicts in the Matabeleland Provinces and some parts of the Midlands Province. Blacks were on blacks. This is still the case in 2020. Blacks are on each other's throats for political reasons. The real reason is that the ZANU-PF party does not want to relinquish power. The Zezuru clan does not want to see any other clan run the country (New Zimbabwe, January 16, 2017).

In South Africa, every type of conflict during the apartheid era erupted in slums, and white areas with heavy human and property losses. Blacks were on blacks, whites were on whites, blacks on whites and whites on blacks. The real reason for these attacks appears to have been resistance to the new changes that were sweeping South Africa. The same applies to other African countries; resistance to any form of change is always challenged very violently.

In the case of South Africa, whites and blacks alike, especially those in privileged positions were more worried about how their privileged positions and their lives would be affected by the changes rather than the wellbeing of society as a whole. Even those who were not satisfied with the system at that time and the conditions under which they worked felt more comfortable with the devil they knew than risk the unknown.

There have also been cases of violent demolition of slums in Nairobi, Kenya, on grounds of state security, cleaning up the 'environment' (city) and giving the land to 'rightful' owners (Rev. Kobia, 1992). In Harare, Zimbabwe, the city authorities demolished slums in the early 1980s primarily to please Queen Elizabeth II who was to visit the country and tour the city. *Murambatsvina* (2005) was another case in

Zimbabwe where many houses were demolished leaving an estimated 700,000 people homeless. The reason given by the government was 'security'.

The real reason, however, was political. Most urban voters had voted for the opposition and needed to be reminded that no one votes for the opposition. While the reasons could be valid at times, the methods used created even more environmental pollution let alone the suffering it brought to the people. The methods used in the cases of Kenya and Zimbabwe cited above involved surprise swoops upon the slum dwellers by a combined force of regular police and the Cities' Security staff supported by bulldozers. The operations were totally inhuman, ruthless and senseless.

The mentality of the architects of such methods of eviction seems not different from those of the colonialists. They painted a picture of slum dwellers as people who were not capable of reasoning the same way colonial Europeans thought of Africans. Is this not a contradiction in value systems? Certainly, slum dwellers and rural people are very well organized within the constraints of their environments under which they live. There are committees with recognized leaders who attend to the slum or rural problems. It is only human that through their leaders they are contacted and prepared for the impending demolition or eviction by providing alternative sites and shelters for them.

The demolitions, which in a few days had rendered hundreds of families homeless, had also affected the education sector very heavily. These also involved the closure and destruction of flea markets and other sites, long used as vending sites by informal traders. Educational services for children were also disrupted. Using force against people, who are defenseless, innocent, victims of political machination, homeless, landless, and unemployed or lowly paid such as slum dwellers and rural squatters, to say the least, is a shame, especially if carried out by authorities that should protect them. Machiavellianism will not solve the problem.

Machiavellianism is one of the traits in what is called the "Dark Triad", the other two being narcissism and psychopathy. The term itself is derived from the infamous Niccolo Machiavelli, a diplomat and philosopher in the Renaissance whose most well-known work became "The Prince" (II Principle). This notorious book espoused his views that strong rulers should be harsh with their subjects and enemies, and that glory and survival justified any means, even ones that were considered immoral and brutal. By the late 16th century, 'Machiavellianism' became a popular word to describe the art of being deceptive to get ahead.

The people we deceive; we must know, are human beings and citizens who are pillars of industrial activities, city services and agricultural production. Christ's concern was for these disadvantaged people in society. The police, city security, staff and the military should only be deployed to assist these people in constructing shelters and infrastructures. This would be one way of improving the environment. City commissioners, municipal and local authorities have the obligation of planning, locating sites and providing social services to these people.

In most of Zimbabwe's cities and towns, service delivery is next to zero because all the money paid to councils and municipalities goes to salaries. City Fathers and their staff must not abdicate their responsibilities. Change must be managed in a proper manner to avoid human loss and environmental disasters. However, due to corruption and mismanagement of funds, this might not be achieved. A change in our way of thinking is needed if we are to make a difference in our towns and cities.

Overcoming resistance to change involves counselling, education and communication, participation by the affected people, giving support by introducing change gradually to give people time to negotiate and adjust. Manipulation and coercion must be kept to a minimum, as they do not give lasting solutions. Sensitivity training, team spirit approach to development, intergroup development, survey and feedback, goal setting, consultation, brainstorming are all-important in change management.

Today, it is important to recognize and promote process oriented multi-disciplinary and holistic approach by overcoming the traditional barriers among and between various disciplines (e.g. government ministries, NGOs, agencies, Universities associations and others).

Secondly, we need to be aware that noble goals on environmental conservation and sustainable development may suffer and be confused by the acceleration of the processes of commercialization. Confusion would also prevail where environmental NGOs, Associations or individuals are involved in the day-to-day decision making with development agencies.

Experience in recent years, shows that it is practically impossible for environmental associations, NGOs and lobbyists to exert pressure on governments or development agencies if their leaders are recruited and integrated by the latter. The work of the environmentalist invariably is clogged up.

Environmental associations or NGOs will make greater achievements and impact if they remain independent and devote themselves more in promoting grass-root social and developmental movements, improving communication with them as well as providing them with material support. This way, they will be effective agents, and will provide checks, and balances in the processes of democratization for greater justice and better living for all.

Thirdly, the interactions between ecological movements and NGOs in Africa and the North need to be sharpened to focus on real problems in the continent so that the Northern based NGOs, or associations use their effectiveness at home to amplify the social, economic and political demands of the African people. Their counterparts in Africa on their part will have to play key roles interacting with the grass-root people and policymakers at all levels to promote environment, and development action-plans and identify new problems that need to be addressed.

In summary, if Africa is to move decisively to tackle environmental issues and embark on sustainable development, then African governments must recognize and act on the following:

1. Establish a framework of governance that stops the wastage of human resources.
2. Overcome inter-ministerial rivalries that hinder multi-disciplinary approaches to problem solving and development.
3. Establish a framework for promoting research based on ecological (i.e. bioregional) networking, and use more indigenous scientists and social workers where available. It is a serious contradiction to criticize the North for bringing wrong technologies to Africa when at the same time promoting the same technologies on the continent. Who runs and funds most of research work in Africa? Certainly, it is not the African governments on their own.
4. African governments should promote and support the activities of independent NGOs (local and international) and religious development agencies, which identify with the people because they are effective organs of change.

5. They must stop speaking publicly about the need for environmental conservation and sustainable development to their people while behind the scenes they compromise for selfish interests and political survival.
6. Africa should establish a framework for meaningful global alliance that will provide solidarity and sharing of views and experiences on environmental protection and sustainable development.
7. Create a framework for environmental leadership training to cover all levels and for developing culturally feasible and efficient technologies.
8. Create a framework for planning in anticipation to provide adequate low-cost shelter, in particular for the slum dwellers and low-income workers, to avoid abrupt and violent demolitions. The framework must ensure that slum dwellers and low-income workers move to the low cost shelters before demolition of slums takes place.
9. Unity, peace and development in diversity should be promoted because if we cannot protect human diversity, then it is unlikely that we can have the capacity to protect plant and have animal diversity.
10. Integrate the press and other media on environmental education.

CHAPTER SIX

THE FINAL

BREAK-THROUGH AND THE FUTURE

"The fault, dear Brutus, is not in our stars, but in ourselves,"

-Shakespeare: Julius Caesar, Act 1, Scene 1

One of the major challenges facing Africa is undoubtedly maintaining a healthy relationship between its people and the environment. Its capacity to protect the environment and establish sustainable development is constrained by the continent's history, culture, ecology, education, institutions, policies, legal framework, politics and level of technology.

Yet Africa must improve the quality of life of its people through maintenance of a cleaner environment, higher incomes, better education, improved nutrition, better health care, equal opportunity, greater individual freedom, improved security and richer cultural life. These can be achieved by re-organizing the vast resources and harnessing them primarily for the benefit of the majority of the people.

Africa must understand that sustainable development and environmental conservation can only be promoted in an atmosphere of peace and stability. Ethnic strife, civil and cross border wars must not be allowed to continue destroying human life in our fragile environment, in which sustainable development is supposed to be rooted.

The process of democratization is slow and the strategies in which government support rather than supplant competitive markets are still far away. These need to be corrected for the good of the continent. On the international scene, the global economic system remains unfavorable, while Africa's debt burden has reached unmanageable proportions. Against this background, a global alliance is still elusive.

However, despite these complex problems, there is still hope for Africa. The final breakthrough will come when the North accepts its share of the blame and take the necessary corrective measures. On its part, Africa must take bold steps to correct internal distortions, which have compounded the continent's problems. Africa is neither poor, nor is its population the primary cause of the continent's underdevelopment.

It is the plundering of its vast wealth, unsustainable lifestyles and wrong development policies, which are the root causes. The continent must arrest her dependence on handouts if it is to develop. It should seek to create circumstances that promote technological co-operation, rather than transfer, as a means of meeting people's material needs.

At present, despite encouraging environmental projects and research efforts, sustainable development is still far away. Wherever some progress is seen, the impulse primarily comes from international organizations or bilateral co-operative arrangements between governments. Only little initiatives come from the people themselves because effective innovations are hardly forth coming from national governments. As already argued in the foregoing chapters, there are specific circumstances to be overcome.

a) Land tenure systems need to be reformed to stimulate progress towards a more permanent strategy, which will eliminate the current state of affairs where individuals or families have very little influence on long-term decisions. When land is controlled by the government, the ruling Party or by a powerful few individuals, the majority have little motivation for environmental protection and sustainable development. This is evident in Zimbabwe where ZANU P.F. thinks it owns the land. As a result, those who own the land are not developing it because they do not know what will happen tomorrow.
b) Capital is another important asset for investment in environmental programmes and sustainable development. The present alarming dependence on money supplies, either in the form of grants or loans from outside will have to be curtailed by promoting

collective self-reliance. African leaders have suddenly woken up to the uncomfortable facts that the shifts by the West to Eastern Europe has meant:

i. Less economic resources available to the continent.
ii. Less investment from the North to Africa.
iii. Less foreign aid to Africa.

The need for collective self-reliance is thus greater now than ever before. The COVID-19 pandemic has compounded the situation.

c) Labor is generally assumed abundant in Africa. This however, is not entirely true. Seasonal distribution is not even and brain drain is alarming. Zimbabwe is a good example. In 2008, Zimbabwe lost many qualified staff such as teachers, nurses, doctors, engineers etc. to Europe and neighboring countries. Quite often, labor is not available at sufficiently low cost. Human resource development is therefore crucial both in terms of skills and availability. This means pragmatic education and adequate incentives.
d) A wealth of knowledge and experience exist in Africa especially in resource management of agrosilvopastoral and pure silvopastoral systems. This potential has not been tapped. It is important to 'rediscover' the existing indigenous experience

and knowledge and put them to good use in resource management. Education should be restructured to meet this need by basing it on the available knowledge, local experience and applied research. The search for knowledge must start at the grass-root level in the village and urban primary schools and move upward. Our understanding of the feedback between ecology, social-economic and socio-cultural processes needed for implementation of environmental progress is still scant. Upgrading of our knowledge is imperative.

e) Sustainable development must be opened to dynamic technical progress. Holistic approach should become an established land-use and industrial concept suitable for spearheading development. The goal should be harmonization of human needs with the environment's life support capacity. The common-bond-integration, harmonization and optimization of land-use and industrial activities, call for inter-disciplinary co-operation.

f) The ultimate challenge is to link environmental protection with development potential that is needed for the livelihood of the present and future generations. This responsibility primarily lies with the policy makers. Scientists, technicians, farmers, urban workers, executive managers, churches and mosques, teachers and social workers play a crucial role in the implementation phase.

g) Africa's key socio-economic weakness remains its inability to think and *'plan ahead'*. The political vices of procrastination, disagreement and governance by telling lies as a political gambit are sinking the continent. Leaders must learn to draw the line between imitation and meeting the aspirations of their people. Politically motivated shortsightedness in dealing with domestic socio-economic issues has to stop.

h) To alleviate the African desire to migrate to the North in search of greener pastures, African governments must value and utilize local talent before rushing for expatriates. The West, on their part, should have a constructive economic development policy to aid the continent to get out of the present economic and environmental problems. Tightening immigration laws is no solution so long as chaos continues to escalate in Africa, more so, if internal conflicts and civil wars are fueled from the North. A clear stand from the North will certainly tame egocentric leaders in

Africa. African leaders on their part should learn to forge unity in cultural diversity and not in conformity.

i) Clearly then, there are responsibilities for the North, Africa and for global alliance in order to achieve the final breakthrough in the continent.

6.1 The Northern Responsibilities

The North and its multinational companies should accept their primary responsibility for Africa's present environmental and economic crisis and implement corrective measures. The decisive test lies in changes in attitudes toward Africans, and their continent by studying and appreciating Africa's sustainable indigenous past. Northern establishments should further undertake economic reforms by establishing fairer commodity prices, reducing protectionism against goods from Africa and by curtailing the plundering habits of its multinational companies of the continent's resources.

The North should also cooperate in the development of environmentally clean and efficient technologies, and stop the dumping of toxic waste on the continent or its waters by its Northern based multinationals. For the North to undertake the above crucial steps, it must put its house in order. This means overcoming current political-economic ills of the 'Northern predicament'. Oystein Tveter in 1991 summed the Northern predicament as follows:

"There is so far no acknowledgement in the North that the fundamental problems lie in the model of how to develop human society which the North is using. The political agenda of the short-term material interests is ruling the day. The process of change in attitude and action is so slow compared with the rapid tempo of the environment and development crisis. The root causes of the problem are left untouched in the best Northern programmes," (SONED 1991).

This Northern predicament regarding the conditions required for achieving environmental protection and sustainable development is likened to the Biblical story of the rich man who asked Jesus what he should do in order to be saved. This is what Jesus said to the rich man: *"You still lack one thing. Sell everything you have and give to the poor, and you will have treasure in heaven. Then come, follow me." When he heard this, he became very sad, because he was very wealthy. Jesus looked at him and said, "How hard it is for the rich to enter the kingdom of God!"* (Luke 18 vs. 22-24 {NIV}).

Stalemate at the earth talks during preparatory meetings in the U.S.A regarding funding for environmental projects in the then Third World by the rich North is a case in point. The problem of the North is that its rulers are so submerged in riches, demanding lifestyles and theology of conquest that they are failing to read the signs of the times. The influx of migrants from Africa into Europe is a sign that all is not well in the world. Immigration laws are only dealing with the symptoms of the problem. What is required is dealing with the problem itself.

6.2 Africa's Responsibility

Africa, a crippled but potential giant, must put its own house in order. Programmes of Northern reform must be matched by fundamental changes in the continent. Africa must recognize indigenous land rights through comprehensive programmes of land reform, not the kind that happened in Zimbabwe. Environmental policies and laws must be strengthened, illegal flight of capital must be stopped and money already in Northern Banks must be returned to the countries of origin for use in development projects it was intended for.

Democratic processes must be encouraged to allow people to become the controllers of their development rather than its passive victims, and gender equality should be promoted.

Above all, inter-regional and national collective self-reliance must be reactivated based on African theology, which embodies useful indigenous traditions, and cultures as well as Christ and Confucius's models. Orchestrated ethnic conflict, civil wars, and corruption all of which are the products of the application of the theology of conquest should be stopped to pave way for stability and peace. These are the pre-requisites for environmental protection and sustainable development.

Positive initiatives from the North should be given an alternative vision for Africa. That means Africa must re-define its understanding of development and proceed to develop production technologies, which are socially, economically and ecologically viable. Finally, Africa must formulate flexible policies and laws that permit greater priority to be given to legitimate basic needs of its people in the interest of survival and living in harmony with nature.

Modern Africans must realize, as their ancestors did, that they live in fragile ecosystems, though rich in resources, and therefore they cannot afford plundering the continent's wealth if they care for the future. They should live within their means, bearing in mind that they do not have the financial resources to tackle the existing and future environmental problems.

Former Nigerian head of state Olusegun Obasanjo once posed this question to Nigerians: *"with such ostentatious living, are we really living like a debtor-nation deserving the sympathy of creditors,"* (AFP Sunday Nation, April 5 1992). He was further reported to have said: *"despite mass poverty in the country and the nation's over 30 billion external debt, there were more luxury cars on Nigerian roads than ever before."* Most African countries have the same syndrome. Living above their means is the cancer cell Africans must remove if they are to get out of the present socio-economic and environmental mess.

6.3 The Joint Endeavour

Regional and global alliances are essential for overall protection of the Earth's resources, but must be based on mutual respect and understanding. The ecological axiom that 'when an ecosystem approaches the limits of its equilibrium, cooperation begins to assume greater value for survival than competition' is true today than ever before. Human beings in their quest for economic development, accumulation of wealth and enjoyment of the riches of nature have tipped the balance of equilibrium in ecosystems in the wrong direction, making a global alliance to arrest the situation and reverse it imperative.

At the grass-root, local community leaders, the clergy, laity and NGOs are better placed to take the lead in sensitizing people, and promoting government policies on the environment and suitable development. Governments on their part must give the necessary support and innovation.

6.4 The writing is on the wall

North and South alike should know that humanity is now under severe time-pressure. The saying, *"they that sin and pray come out clean"* will not do. We are all in the common spaceship: earth. If it crash-lands because of the misconduct of a few, we shall all perish. Difficult as it may be to abandon old habits, human beings must take a bold step to *"go through a narrow gate that leads to life and abandon the wide gate that leads to destruction."* Indeed, *"the gate to life is narrow and the way that leads to it is hard; and there are few people who find it,"* (Matthew 7 vs. 13-14 {NET}). Let the few who find it begin and show the way to the many still searching for it.

African leaders, bureaucrats, technocrats, and NGOs are faced with two options. Either to take a step to follow the hard road that leads to the narrow gate of life to save human beings from the looming catastrophe or gravitate towards the wide and easy going road of political and economic expediency (i.e. path of compromise) and face the onslaught by nature and its Creator. In that war, human beings are certain to be the great losers. So let us be advised!

Let me add that, although inflation, hunger, disease, poverty, murder, rape, terrorism, civil wars, ethnic conflicts and corruption are already posing threats to human beings, if governance issues and the blame game are not addressed by African leaders the future of the continent will be very bleak for all.

If African leaders succumb to the persuasion or pressure from the cornucopian, then human beings will increasingly lose their mental capacity to understand the complexities of life, because our creative impulses will be hitting more and more dead ends, as humanity will be coming under more attack from nature on so many varied fronts. The hitherto benign climate will turn hostile, good top soils will disappear more rapidly, deforestation will accelerate, aquatic life will diminish at an alarming rate and there will be no time to adapt. That will logically lead to greater confusion, conflicts, wars and finally human extinction. The future is now or never. The choice is ours!

GLOSSARY

NB: *This section only defines indistinct terms found within the principal text of this book.*

Agenda 21

Agenda 21 is the plan of action to achieve sustainable development that was adopted by the world leaders at the United Nations Conference on Environment and Development held in Rio De Janeiro, Brazil in June 1992. Its aim is to achieve global sustainable development. Sustainable development is the idea that human societies must live and meet their needs without comprising the ability of future generations to meet their own needs.

One of the major objectives of Agenda 21 initiative is that every local government should draw its own local Agenda 21. Local Agenda 21 is a voluntary process of local community consultation with the aim of creating local policies and programmes that work towards achieving sustainable development. Local Agenda 21 encompasses awareness raising, capacity building, community participation and the formation of partnerships. These are the hallmarks of any development process.

In summary, Agenda 21 is a comprehensive plan of action to be taken globally nationally and locally by organizations of the United Nations system, governments and major groups in every area in which humans impact on the environment. It is important because it requires all nations to take action towards climate change, reduce unemployment, strengthen gender equality and promote peaceful societies, if the world is to eradicate poverty and shift into a more sustainable development.

G-7

This is an informal bloc of the seven industrialized democracies that meets annually to discuss global issues such as security, energy, development etc. The eleven countries in the bloc are Canada, France, Germany, Italy, Japan, United Kingdom and the United States of America. The bloc was found in 1997.

G-77

The Group of 77 (G77) at the United Nations is a coalition of 134 developing countries, designed to promote its members' collective economic interests and create an enhanced joint negotiating capacity in the United Nations.

Its founding was the result of a collective perception on their most common problems. These countries had also recognized the need for joint action in accordance with the principles and objectives of the United Nations' Charter, in the face of the inequitable pattern of international development. It was founded at Geneva, Switzerland by 77 countries; hence, the name G-77.

BIBLIOGRAPHY

Alabaster, J. S. (1981). Review of the state of aquatic pollution of East African inland waters CIFA Occa Pap. (9): 36.

Albertyn, R. and P. Daniels (2009). Research within the context of Community Engagement.

Bone, J. D.et al. (1977). Trees, food and people. Ottawa IDRC.

Besse-brakenfield, P. (1991). United Nations Conference on Environment and Development: NGO play an important role. Gate No. 3 1/91 December.

Biney, C.A. et al. Scientific Bases for pollution Control in African Inland Waters. Chemistry and Ecology Volume 3 No. 1 1991.

Brown, L. (1990). In Environmental Accounting: Putting a value on natural resources: by John Laird, 1991: Our planet Volume 3 No. 1, 1991.

Elson, M. J. (1986). Greenbelt: Conflict Mediation in the Urban Fringe. London. Heinemann.

Fadaka, J.O. (1992). Local Communities and Biodiversity. In: Daily Nation Jan 16, 1992.
FAO (1976). Forest for research Development, FAO Rome.

Fisher-Thompson, J. (1992). Can Africa's military be a guardian of pluralism? In: Daily Nairobi Jan 10, 1992.

Hitchcock B (1992. How not to rule a country. In: Daily Nation March 24, 1992.

IDFNA (1991). International Decade on Food and Nutrition for Africa-Programme Proposal 1992-2002.

King, K. F. S. (1968). Agri-silviculture Bulletin No. 1 department of Forestry, University of Ibadan, Nigeria.

King, K. F. S. (1987). Agroforestry: a decade of development.

Kizito, R. (1992). Forging Unity and Cultural Liberation, Personal Communication.

Kobia, Rev., (1992) Demolitions: What next? Nairobi

Loughran, G. (1992) Tanzania: The potential of a slumbering giant. In: Daily Nairobi April 17, 1992

Von Magdelil H. J. (1987) Agroforestry in the dry zones of Africa: past, present and future in Agroforestry: a decade of development.

Mazrui, A. A. (1986) The Africans: A triple Heritage. BBC Publ. 1986.

Mazrui, A. A. (1992) Global apartheid in the new World Order: In: Sunday Nation February 2, 1992

MacNamara, R. S. (1973) One hundred countries, two million people. New York: Praege.

Merchant, J. A. (1989) Implication of occupational and environmental Health from use of Agricultural Technology, Nairobi 1992.

Mkangi, K. (1990) The Debt Crisis. ACLCA Publ. Nairobi.

M'Mwereria, G. K. (1990) The Root causes of Debt Crisis in Africa: An Agenda for Continental Collective Self-reliance.

Muslim, A. F. (1975) The Land and References Environment in Kenya. Nairobi, University of Nairobi Thesis.

Obudho, R. A. et al (1991) Urban Environmental Problems in Kenya. Conference Paper, Nairobi, 19-23 August 1991.

Ojo, G. J. A. (1966) Yoruba Culture, University of Ife and London Press.

Ojwang, J.B. (1992) Environmental Law and Political Change In Kenya, Nairobi.

Othello-Gruduah (1972) Putting Environmental First, In: Standard April 5, 1992.

Nyerere, J (1985) African's Place in the World. Symp. Wellesley College UK. 1985.

Prowse, M (1985) I.M.F: A Capitalist tool in need of sharpening. In: Daily Nation March 10, 1992.

Sakari, W. D. O. (1989). Occupational Hazards: An Overview of the Kenya situation. Nairobi Soned (1991). SONED ON UNCED: A Southern Network for Development (SONED) African Region.

Sunday News (1992) President Bush rejects global warming targets. In the Sunday News March 29, 1992.

Sunday News (1992) Showy Nigerians anger Obasanjo, In: Sunday Nation Feb 9, 1992.

Standard (1992) World Bank reacts to 'dirty' memo.

Daily Nation (1992) World Bank denies plans to dump waste in Africa. In: Daily Nation Feb 9, 1992.

Tolba, M. (1991) Fourth Session of the Inter-govenmental Negotiating Committee for Conservation of Biodiversity, Nairobi-Kenya Sept 22, 1991.

UNCHS (Habitat) (1988) Refuse Collection vehicles for Developing Countries, Nairobi (UNCHS).

UNCHS (Habitat) (1987) Global report on Human Settlements. New York: Oxford University Press.

UNDP (1992) Human Development Report 1992. In: Daily Nation, May 5, 1992.

West, W. Q. B. and Biney C. A. (1991) African Fisheries and the Environment, FAO RAFR Publication

Westoby, J. (1975) Forest Industries for socio-economic development. Y. Coedwigwr No. 31.

W. T. B. T. S. (1990) Mankind's search for God. Publ. Watchtower Bible and Tract Society of Pennsylvania, N.Y. USA.

www.ingramcontent.com/pod-product-compliance
Lightning Source LLC
LaVergne TN
LVHW012330100826
845148LV00017B/1907